D1519980

Screenplay Library
Edited by Matthew J. Bruccoli

THE ASPHALT JUNGLE

A Screenplay
By Ben Maddow
and John Huston
From a novel by W. R. Burnett

Afterword by W. R. Burnett

Southern Illinois University Press
Carbondale and Edwardsville

Feffer & Simons, Inc.
London and Amsterdam

Library of Congress Cataloging in Publication Data

Maddow, Ben, 1909-
  The asphalt jungle.

  (Screenplay library)
  I. Huston, John, 1906-   II. Burnett,
William Riley, 1899-   The asphalt jungle.
III. Title. IV. Series.
PN1997.A78   1980   812'.54   79-26729
ISBN 0-8093-0942-4
ISBN 0-8093-0946-7 pbk.

Contents

Foreword

Although it now has classic status, *The Asphalt Jungle* was not a box-office hit when released in 1950. The reception may have been muddied by reviewers who complained that the criminals were too sympathetic. Bosley Crowther of the *New York Times* was particularly distressed by what he obscurely called "the item of repulsive exhibition." He lamented, "If only it all weren't so corrupt!"

One of the distinctions of this screenplay is that it turns cops-and-robbers types into characters. This process was abetted by splendid performances from Louis Calhern, Sam Jaffe, Sterling Hayden, James Whitmore, and Jean Hagen. John Huston's step-by-step direction of the mechanics of the robbery—which was then an innovation—has become a commonplace of crime caper movies, achieving its most celebrated treatment in *Rififi* (1955). Another gauge of the influence that *The Asphalt Jungle* has had on other movies is that it has been re-made—badly—three times: *The Badlanders* (1958), *Cairo* (1963), and *Cool Breeze* (1972).

The Asphalt Jungle was nominated for best screenplay by the Motion Picture Academy and for best-written American drama by the Writers Guild. John Huston was also nominated for best director by the Academy.

M.J.B.

Acknowledgments

The editor is grateful for the generous help of Herbert S. Nusbaum of Metro-Goldwyn-Mayer. Mrs. Ben Hamilton of Hampton Books provided the illustrations.

The Asphalt Jungle

Credits

Screenplay by Ben Maddow and John Huston from a novel by W. R. Burnett. Art directors, Cedric Gibbons and Randall Duell. Photography, Harold Rosson. Editor, George Boemer. Sound, Douglas Shearer. Produced by Arthur Hornblow, Jr., for MGM. Directed by John Huston. Running time: 112 minutes.

Cast

Dix Handley	Sterling Hayden
Alonzo D. Emmerich	Louis Calhern
Doll Conovan	Jean Hagen
Gus Minissi	James Whitmore
Doc Erwin Riedenschneider	Sam Jaffe
Commissioner Hardy	John McIntire
Cobby	Marc Lawrence
Lieutenant Ditrich	Barry Kelley
Louis Ciavelli	Anthony Caruso
Maria Ciavelli	Teresa Celli
Angela	Marilyn Monroe
Timmons	William Davis
May Emmerich	Dorothy Tree
Bob Brannom	Brad Dexter
Dr. Swanson	John Maxwell

The
Asphalt Jungle

FADE IN:

EXT LONG SHOT CITY STREET IN A POOR NEIGHBORHOOD NIGHT
in a vast, sprawling midwestern city. Far down the street, almost at the end of the vista, a police car cruising at ten miles per hour creeps slowly toward the CAMERA. The occupants are not yet visible, but we are aware of voices distorted through a radio speaker, official voices often overlapping, in which pieces of words and numbers are sometimes distinguishable. The car continues to move, keeping close to the curb. The asphalt road, the cement sidewalks, the dark store windows and brick sides of the four-or five-story tenements, are now all the same color and texture: wet, black, and shiny—for a fine rain has been falling all day and all evening.

Still moving slowly and steadily toward the CAMERA, its radio a little louder, though not any clearer, is the police prowl car. It is close enough now to see two officers in the front seat.

MEDIUM TRUCKING SHOT CITY STREET ANGLE AS IF FROM THE POLICE CAR
The dark store fronts swing around, the corner is slowly turned, the new vista is spotted now with the neon invitations of a dozen bars. As they drive slowly by, the music—rhumba and hillbilly—drowns out for a moment the official voices of the police radio.

MEDIUM SHOT CITY STREET

PANNING with the police car as it comes to the end of the block and enters a short vehicular tunnel, an archway lined with porcelain brick.

MEDIUM TRUCKING SHOT INSIDE VEHICULAR TUNNEL ANGLE AS IF FROM THE POLICE CAR
An elderly man with a stooped walk is approached and overtaken

3

4   The Asphalt Jungle

by another much younger and better-dressed man. He walks alongside him and there is an urgent, whispered offer—it is impossible to tell of what—but the elderly man shakes his head. The younger man abandons his customer and turning his face away from the invisible, slowly moving police car, scratches a light on the porcelain brick.

MEDIUM LONG SHOT   CITY STREET   AS THE POLICE CAR
emerges from the short tunnel, its radio speaker still muttering methodically.

MEDIUM TRUCKING SHOT   CITY STREET   ANGLE AS IF FROM THE POLICE CAR
which is passing through a street of rooming houses, whose outer doors open directly on the level of the sidewalk. Most are shut and dark, but in one there is the shadow of a couple, the man a little drunk and trying his fist on the smudged glass of the door, the woman raising both hands to restrain him. More silent houses, then, a little farther along, a door is flung open and a young woman bursts out into the street. One shoe is broken and torn. She has no hat, and she is crying, as much out of anger as anything else. Her face comes quite close by the CAMERA, and she pulls at the white satin scarf around her neck as if it were choking her.

MEDIUM LONG SHOT   CITY STREET   AS THE POLICE CAR
its radio still going, turns another corner and descends a narrow cobblestone street toward the river.

MEDIUM LONG SHOT   CITY STREET
as the police car crawls along the river front, moving toward the mass of a black bridge outlined with cords of light. The radio VOICES continue.

MEDIUM TRUCKING SHOT   ANGLE AS IF FROM THE POLICE CAR PAST A CEMENT PARAPET AND TOWARD THE RIVER
The sleek, oily black surface, rippled by the wind, carries along something yellowish white and indistinguishable. The object floats closer and downstream into the reflection of light from the bridge. It's clear for a moment before it passes back into the shadow—it's only a crate from the long wholesale piers at the edge of the city.

MEDIUM SHOT   STREET ALONG THE RIVER FRONT

CAMERA PANNING with police car. The radio voice is silent for a moment, then reports much more closely and therefore more clearly.

POLICE RADIO OPERATOR
(O.S.)
Attention 71A—a holdup, Hotel de Paris, Camden Square—repeat, holdup, Hotel de Paris—

The police car turns, spurts forward and up a short hill away from the river.

MEDIUM TRUCKING SHOT A NARROW CITY STREET SEEN THROUGH THE WINDSHIELD OF THE POLICE CAR
The street is lined with the closed iron doors of silent warehouses. After two short blocks, taken with increasing speed, the street ends in a squalid triangle with a single area of light: the open stairway to the Hotel de Paris. (The sign above the entrance reads: $1.00 WITH RUNNING WATER.) The police car races toward the hotel.

DISSOLVE TO:

EXT MEDIUM SHOT CITY STREET NIGHT

CAMERA PANS RIGHT TO FOLLOW a tall man in a rumpled suit and a wide-brimmed hat. The hat, the slow walk, the man himself, are more characteristic of a small town in the South or the Southwest than of this raw, Midwest industrial city. The man turns, entering a hamburger stand. Chipped enameled letters on the window identify it as: GUS' ALL-NITE.

INT MEDIUM CLOSE SHOT HAMBURGER STAND NIGHT
as the man enters from the wet street outside. He turns to a newsstand and picks out two newspapers and a *Racing Form*. The CAMERA BEGINS TO PULL BACK REVEALING the proprietor standing behind the counter wiping his hands on a towel. He has short, thick, powerful arms, heavy shoulders and a fat torso. He is Gus Minissi, a grinning, jovial hunchback.

The tall man, Dix, looks up at him through his narrow eyes. He has the face of a farmer or a river pilot. Harsh, lean, forceful, there is something about the bones of his face which is a little alien, as if he had an ancestor who was part Indian.

Behind Dix, but visible to Gus through the front window, two
policemen in their wet rubber capes are coming across the street
toward the door of the hamburger stand.

MEDIUM CLOSE TWO-SHOT   GUS AND DIX
Dix hands a heavy, nickel-plated revolver across the counter to Gus.
Gus puts it under the counter. The two officers enter.

MEDIUM SHOT   DIX   IN F.G.
as one of the officers searches him. Gus moves away in the B.G.,
turning to adjust the lights under his hamburger grill.

                    OLDER OFFICER
        Gus—when did this punk come in here?

                        GUS
        Don't ask me. I don't look at the clock—I own this place.

                    YOUNGER OFFICER
                (completing his search of Dix)
        No gun—no money—no nothing—

OLDER OFFICER

Search the place.

GUS

Got a warrant?

YOUNGER OFFICER

Look, Gus, why don't you cooperate?

GUS

Get a warrant.

OLDER OFFICER
(taking hold of Dix's arm)
All right—take him in.

YOUNGER OFFICER

What on?

OLDER OFFICER

We'll book him on vag—the night cashier got a good look
at him, this time.

The two officers take Dix out of the hamburger stand and toward the
prowl car.

DISSOLVE TO:

MEDIUM CLOSE SHOT   POLICE LINE-UP ROOM   EARLY MORN-
ING   SEVERAL BLINDING LIGHTS
directly into CAMERA. The CAMERA SWINGS DOWN REVEAL-
ING in the F.G. the backs of the heads of ten or so men in the early
morning police line-up. The room, about one-half full of officers and
plainclothesmen shifting about on wooden chairs, is just visible
beyond the lights. In the front row, already bored and frowning, sits
the massive, tough Lieutenant Ditrich.

DITRICH

All right, Jack, go ahead.

MEDIUM SHOT   POLICE LINE-UP ROOM
At the left stands the police clerk who has just been addressed by
Lieutenant Ditrich. Bald, coughing, he shuffles the records in his
hands.

                              JACK
                    (reading)
              Smith, Karl Anton—age 47.

MEDIUM CLOSE SHOT　THE FIRST MAN IN THE LINE-UP
He is a dull, heavy, stolid man.

                              JACK
                    (O.S.)
              Arrested 6 P.M. last night. Phoned police station, stating
              he had murdered Mrs. Katherine Smith.

MEDIUM CLOSE SHOT　POLICE CLERK
Shuffles another set of records.

MEDIUM CLOSE SHOT　SECOND MAN IN THE LINE-UP
He has a thin nose, a narrow, cramped, sweating forehead and
hyper-thyroid eyes.

                              JACK
                    (O.S.)
              Goldy, William—age 22. Possession narcotics. Occu-
              pation—clerk—no previous record. Attempt suicide last
              night with necktie.

With a gesture which it is impossible for him to resist, the man
touches his bony fingers to his throat.

CAMERA MOVES RIGHT into MEDIUM CLOSE SHOT of DIX.

                              JACK
                    (O.S.)
              Handley, William Tuttle alias "Dix" Handley. Born Ken-
              tucky. Occupation—none. Age 36. Arrested 1935—
              loitering—no disposition. Arrested 1937—illegal posses-
              sion firearms. Sentence 1 to 5.

MEDIUM SHOT　DITRICH LOUNGING IN THE FRONT ROW

                              JACK
                    (O.S.)
              Escaped State Prison—1939. Arrested 1940. Released 1943.
              September 1943—arrested suspicion armed robbery—no
              disposition. 1946, arrested suspicion armed robbery. No
              disposition.
Lieutenant Ditrich fidgets in the front row.

JACK
(O.S., his voice continuing the record of Dix's arrest)
1947—arrested suspicion assault and robbery. Acquitted.
1948—

DITRICH
(interrupting)
Is that night clerk here?
A studious man with thinning hair stands up in the front row.

NIGHT CLERK
Yes, sir.

DITRICH
Hotel de Paris?

NIGHT CLERK
Yes, sir.

DITRICH
Well, do you see the man who pulled the stick-up last
night?

NIGHT CLERK
I . . . I don't know . . .

DITRICH
What do you mean you don't know?

NIGHT CLERK
(timidly)
His hat was on . . .

DITRICH
(gesturing to the line-up)
Put on your hats!

MEDIUM SHOT   THE MEN IN THE LINE-UP
putting on their hats.

DITRICH
(O.S.)
Well?

CLOSE SHOT   NIGHT CLERK
He shifts nervously, staring at Dix.

CLOSE SHOT DIX
looking at the night clerk, his face terrifying because of his lack of expression.

> DITRICH
> (O.S.)
> He was tall, you say—he had on a brown suit—and a wide-brim hat. He had heavy eyebrows.
> (furiously)
> All right, don't you see him?

CLOSE SHOT NIGHT CLERK
He looks at Dix without a word.

CLOSE SHOT DITRICH

> DITRICH
> (to Dix)
> What's your name?

CLOSE SHOT DIX
He pauses a moment before replying. His gaze remains fixed on the night clerk.

> DIX
> Handley.

> DITRICH
> (O.S.)
> Full name!

> DIX
> William Tuttle Handley.

There is in his voice, not so much a drawl as a slur, a Southern softening of speech, but spoken between barely opened lips.

> DITRICH
> (O.S.)
> Where'd you get the name—Dix?

> DIX
> That's what they call me.

CLOSE SHOT DITRICH
scowling at Dix. Then he turns on the night clerk.

DITRICH
Well, come on—is that the man?

CLOSE SHOT   NIGHT CLERK
stared down by Dix.

NIGHT CLERK
No . . . it isn't . . . him.

MEDIUM SHOT   POLICE LINE-UP ROOM   LIEUTENANT DITRICH IN
THE FRONT ROW.
He gets up to stare with fury at the reluctant witness. Before he can
say anything, a young sergeant approaches him.

SERGEANT
I got a message from Commissioner Hardy, sir.

DITRICH
(snapping at him)
What is it?

SERGEANT
Wants to see you in his office in half an hour.
Ditrich stares at him, beginning to sweat.

DISSOLVE TO:

INT   FULL SHOT   POLICE COMMISSIONER HARDY'S OFFICE   DAY
Hardy stands at the window, looking out in silence. He is a short
man, with white hair and an owl's beak and some of the owl's real
ferocity. Lieutenant Ditrich, standing, waits for him to speak.
Hardy slowly turns from the window and glares at him.

HARDY
Thirty-nine thefts, thirty-three burglaries, eighteen rob-
beries, seven assaults, five morals offenses in the last
thirty days. That's a record—even for the Fourth Precinct,
Lieutenant Ditrich.

DITRICH
We know the guy that's been pulling most of the stick-
ups, Commissioner—name's Dix Handley. He was in the
show-up this morning, but our witness got cold feet and
backed down. What can you do?

HARDY

Lock up the witness. Scare him worse. It's your job knowing what to do. As things are, the only merchants who are
safe from harm are the ones who take wagers on the
horses.
        (shakes his finger into Ditrich's face)
I want to know why those parlors are still operating.

DITRICH

I close them down, but they only open up again.

HARDY

You don't close them hard enough. Tear the phones out!
Break the furniture up!

DITRICH

People like to bet the horses, sir, and just because the law
says no . . .

HARDY

        (furious)
I don't want your opinion of the law!
There is a long silence then:

DITRICH

        Is that all, sir?
Hardy goes to his desk, picks up a folder, gestures with it.

HARDY

No. That's not all. Where's Erwin Riedenschneider?

DITRICH

I'm waiting to hear on that, sir.

HARDY

You don't know where he is, do you?

DITRICH

No, sir, but we ought to get word from our stoolies . . .

HARDY

It was all dumped in your lap. He left State Prison yesterday at twelve noon—took a train to this city—time of
arrival: three-seventeen. All you had to do was spot him,
and stay on his tail for twenty-four hours;—after which

.

time, if he failed to register, we'd lock him up. What happens? He loses you six blocks from the depot! And one of the most dangerous criminals alive is now at large in this city.

DITRICH

The two men on that detail ought to get medals for dumbness.

HARDY

They were assigned by you, so you deserve one too.— Ditrich, I can do three things about you: I can reduce you to the rank of patrolman and send you out to Five Corners—or I can bring you up for departmental trial on charge of incompetence—or I can give you one more chance to live up to your responsibilities—and that's what I'm going to do. Maybe that's the worst punishment of all.

DISSOLVE TO:

INT   CLOSE SHOT   TAXI   NIGHT
In the F.G., the creased, thick, shaven back of a man's neck and hat—a black homburg. The driver glances around at him.

DRIVER

You're sure you know where you're going, Buddy?
(the fare nods)
It's none of my business, partner, but this is a rough neighborhood.

The taxi stops. CAMERA PULLS BACK to reveal "Doc" Riedenschneider—short, dumpy, middle-aged. He gets out of the cab, carrying a small suitcase.

DRIVER

There's the number you're looking for, but it's dark. Want me to wait?

Doc places the suitcase on the sidewalk beside him, pays the driver then picks up the suitcase and TURNS INTO CAMERA.

DRIVER

I wouldn't go parading around with a suitcase. Some of these young punks would clip you . . .

EXT   MEDIUM SHOT   CITY STREET   NIGHT
Toward the back of the Doctor as he approaches a dark store front,
entirely vacant except for a tobacco advertisement abandoned in the
front window.

                         DRIVER
              (O.S.)
         . . . just to get a clean shirt.
The Doc, without comment, looks for, finds, presses a buzzer. It
sounds far away, deep inside the store.

INT   MEDIUM SHOT   NIGHT   FROM INSIDE THE EMPTY STORE
The Doc waits outside the door, buzzes again. In the B.G., seen
through the dusty window, the driver goes off up the empty street.
There is a SOUND of footsteps scraping toward the door; then the
door is opened the three inches that the chain will permit by
Timmons, doorman to this odd establishment, a hulking, bull-
necked man with clipped blond hair.

                         TIMMONS
         Yeah?

                         DOC
         I want to see Cobby.

                         TIMMONS
         Who are you?

                         DOC
              (patiently)
         Just tell him, Doc is here and would like to see him.
Timmons considers this another second. There is the faint CLANK
of a chain, then Timmons opens the door enough for the little man
to squeeze through.

INT   DARK CORRIDOR
There are several doors in the corridor. From beyond them comes
the SOUND of voices and the CLINK of poker chips.

                         TIMMONS
         Wait here.
              (he goes down the hall, to a door)
         You better be legit, pal. Cobby's been having trouble

lately, and he ain't so easy to get along with—not that he ever was.

He opens the door and enters. Almost immediately, the door flies open and a little ferret of a man in shirt sleeves bounds out into the hall.

> COBBY
>
> Well, where the devil is he?

He stands in a pool of light cast from the room. Timmons indicates the Doc, who starts forward. Cobby meets him halfway.

> COBBY
>
> All right—make it fast. I'm a busy man. What do you want?

> DOC
>
> I just got out today.

> COBBY
>
> Oh. So that's it. I'm getting tired of you guys that fell putting the bite on me. I'm no First National Bank.

> DOC
>
> I got a proposition for you.

> COBBY
>
> (irritably)
> All you guys have.

> DOC
>
> Maybe you didn't get who I was . . .

> COBBY
>
> (dancing with impatience)
> I never seen you before. Come on, what is it?

> DOC
>
> Maybe you've heard of me. The Professor . . . Herr Doktor, maybe?

Cobby's mouth drops. He stares in astonishment. After a pause:

> COBBY
>
> You mean you are Riedenschneider?

Doc nods.

                    COBBY
          Well, why didn't you say so?
Cobby glares at Timmons, then bounds into the little office at the
end of the corridor. Although he's in his middle forties, he moves
around like a high school kid—always nervous, geared-up, always
irritable. Taking off his homburg, Doc follows.

INT   OFFICE

                    COBBY
          Sit down, Doc. Have a drink.
                    (he opens a drawer—produces a bottle)

                    DOC
          Nothing to drink. I got out of the habit behind the Walls.
          That's all it is—a habit.
He pulls back his lips in what is intended for a smile, but his face
remains expressionless. Cobby, still dancing about, pours himself a
long one.

                    COBBY
          Here's to the drink habit. It's the only one I got that don't
          get me into trouble. What's on your mind, Doc?

                    DOC
          I got a proposition—a big one.

                    COBBY
          How big is big?

                    DOC
          Too big for you, Cobby.
Cobby dances about under the stimulus of injured pride.

                    COBBY
          Now wait, Doc. I don't like to brag, but I'm doing all right
          making book. I'm in the chips. What kind of proposition
          is it?

                    DOC
          A plan for a caper. And it's a good one. I could sell it for
          one hundred thousand dollars on the open market. But
          that would be throwing money away. I prefer to execute it
          myself and make—
                    (he pauses)

COBBY
(breathless)
How much?

DOC
Half a million dollars.

Cobby swallows painfully, stares at Doc for a long moment, then he gulps his drink and pours another with a shaking hand.

COBBY
I know when you talk, Doc, it ain't through your hat.

DOC
Of course, I will have to do a little checking—as the plan is some years old—but not much checking—not much. I'll need—roughly, fifty thousand to operate.

COBBY
(wiping his face with a silk handkerchief)
That ain't chicken feed—

DOC
I told you.

COBBY
As a rule I could handle it, but . . . well . . . the Happiness Boys just paid me a call, and I'm left short . . . fifty thousand . . . I don't see . . .

DOC
Of course. I thought maybe Mr. Emmerich . . .

COBBY
What do you know about Mr. Emmerich?

DOC
Only what I heard in the Walls. That he has money to invest, and that the way to get to him is through you.
(he stands)
Of course if the information is not correct . . .

COBBY
Correct—sure it's correct. It's just I never thought of Mr. Emmerich in connection with this kind of a deal. Sit down, Doc. Excuse me for a moment. I'll be right back.

He dances out of the room. The Doc puffs his cigar, rises and examines a Vargas cutie on a wall calendar. Interested, he lifts the page to see the girl on the next month. Someone comes to the open door. Expecting to see Cobby, the Doc glances up. Dix stands there. Doc regards the tall, raw-boned, dark-faced man. Without a word, Dix turns to leave, but at that moment Cobby appears.

> COBBY
>
> Hello, Dix. What do you want?

Dix glances at the little Doctor.

> DIX
>
> I want to make a bet.

He has a slight southern accent.

> COBBY
>
> Well?

> DIX
>
> Your man says you got to o.k. it.

> COBBY
>
> What are you in for?

> DIX
>
> Twenty-three hundred and some.

> COBBY
>
> (after a pause)
>
> Okay. You're tab's good to twenty-five hundred. But that's the limit. Either pick a winner or pay me when you get that far.

Something happens to Dix's face—the brows meet and the jaw muscles swell. His dark eyes become fierce. Cobby backs up a step.

> DIX
>
> (in a low quiet voice)
>
> Don't bone me.

> COBBY
>
> (fearfully)
>
> I'm not boning you, Dix.

> DIX
>
> Did I ever welch?

COBBY
Nobody said you did.

DIX
You just boned me.

COBBY
Look, Dix—I only said . . .

DIX
(evenly)
I'm not asking favors. I'll go get you that twenty-three hundred right now.

He turns abruptly, goes out the door, and down the hall. Cobby dances after him pleading:

COBBY
Dix—Dix—Listen to me. Come back—Have a drink.

The outer door can be heard slamming. Cobby comes back into the room.

MEDIUM TWO-SHOT   DOC AND COBBY

COBBY
(loudly, as if to bolster up his courage)
Can you beat that? Where does he come off . . . blowing a fuse—

DOC
Who is he?

COBBY
Oh, a small time hooligan who's crazy for horses. My book beats him and beats him, but he keeps coming back for more.

He pours again quickly.

COBBY
(laughs)
Say, Doc, I almost forgot on account of that big tramp. Mr. Emmerich's going to talk to us later tonight. He and his wife are giving a dinner party at his house in town. They know all the swells. But he'll be at another address later on.

(Cobby winks)
A man like Mr. Emmerich has more than one place to hang
his hat.

DISSOLVE TO:

INT   MEDIUM SHOT   GUS'S HAMBURGER JOINT   NIGHT
A truck driver stands at the magazine rack, eating a king-sized
hamburger and stealing looks at the girl pictures in a movie magazine. The cat jumps onto the counter and Gus starts feeding him
meat, bite by bite. Dix enters. He and Gus exchange nods. Dix takes
a seat at the counter.

                    GUS
Smart cat . . . Never does a lick of work. Out all night.
Sleeps all day . . .

                    TRUCK DRIVER
What's a big, dirty cat doing at a eating place? I run over
one every time I get a chance. People feeding cats when
some kids can't get enough to eat!

                    GUS
          (quietly)
You gonna buy that magazine?

                    TRUCK DRIVER
          (laughs)
Why should I? I seen all the dames already. Want to make
something of it?

                    GUS
A little off your beat, ain't you, buster?

                    TRUCK DRIVER
How do you mean, Humpty-Dumpty?

                    GUS
I mean you don't belong around here. You're just passing
          through—only not fast enough.
Gus comes around the counter with surprising speed. He seizes the
truck driver by the arm; whirls him around; grabs the seat of his
pants; jerks it up tight until the bit fellow is on his tip-toes; then
"Spanish walks" him swiftly to the front door, where he gives the
flabbergasted driver a push.

GUS

(shouting)

And if I ever see you running over a cat, I'll kick your teeth out.

The driver stands staring at Gus, trying to recover from the surprise attack. He is unable to make up his mind whether to clout the little hunchback or beat a dignified retreat.

TRUCK DRIVER

I'd take you apart if you were a foot taller, and straightened out a little.

Gus steps toward the driver, carrying his hands low. The driver hurriedly gets into his truck. Gus comes back into his joint. Dix watches Gus turn the lock in the door, and pull the window blinds. Dix is smiling for a change.

GUS

I suppose you want your heater back? Well, you ain't goin' to get it! What do you think of that?

DIX

Quit kidding, Gus!

GUS

I mean it . . .

Dix stops smiling.

GUS

Go ahead—get sore—smack me down—

MEDIUM CLOSE TWO-SHOT   DIX AND GUS

Dix reaches out, takes a toothpick.

DIX

You know I wouldn't do that, Gus.

GUS

Dix, take my advice. Knock off for a while. The Happiness Boys are on the rampage. Headquarters is giving them the push.

DIX

I can't afford to knock off.

GUS

Stop worrying. I'll stake you.

DIX

I need twenty-three hundred.

GUS

What!

DIX

There's something I just got to take care of.

GUS

. . . Cobby maybe . . . ?

Dix nods.

GUS

Let him sweat, it'll do him good. Cobby can spare a few
pounds.

DIX

(shakes his head)

You can't owe money to a guy like him. A little loudmouth
who bones you when he isn't even trying to.

GUS

I don't get you, Dix.

DIX

I just can't be in Cobby's debt and keep my self-respect.

GUS

(groans)

All right. I got a grand put away—you can have that, and
maybe I can dig up thirteen hundred more . . . I guess it's
all right to owe me money.

DIX

(grins slowly)

I guess . . .

GUS

Just my luck . . . I'll have it for you tomorrow or bust a gut.
In the meantime, stay away from the boulevard—specially
at night . . . oh, by the way—they knocked over that clip
joint—the Club Royal—wasn't that where Doll worked?

DIX

Yeah.

(he laughs a strange, mirthless sound)
It's coming in bunches it looks like.

GUS

Go home, Dix. Stay home. And don't get your flag at half-mast. You still got old Gus.

Dix looks at Gus. He'd like to thank him, Gus would like to be thanked, but neither man is used to gratitude. Dix goes out of the stand, crossing the street and walking slowly and calmly out of the square. In the F.G., Gus begins to dial a number on the wall phone.

DISSOLVE TO:

INT   FULL SHOT   LOUIS CIAVELLI'S BEDROOM   NIGHT

It is a small room, crowded with relatively new furniture, whose outlines—especially those of the big double bed and the bars of a baby's crib close by—are visible in the light of a street arc outside. The phone is RINGING behind the closed door of the hall. The baby in the crib gives a fretful cry. Maria, a full-bodied, plump young woman, stirs under the covers; then waking, lifts herself far enough to reach a bar of the crib and shake it gently, rocking the baby back to sleep.

MARIA

The phone, Louis!

Louis sits up in bed. He is a young man with a pale handsome face, dark eyes, and black hair just beginning to thin out at the forehead. He yawns widely and scratches his head. The phone continues to RING.

MARIA

Get it, Louis, get it.

Louis gets out of bed and hurries out of the room. The CAMERA STAYS ON Maria, rocking the baby in its crib. Gradually, with a little mournful cry, the baby begins to go to sleep.

LOUIS

Yeah?—for crying out loud, Gus. You know what time it is? Must be two o'clock . . . What do you want, Gus? . . . How much? . . . Thirteen hundred! . . . You must be crazy! . . . For Dix?—What do I care about that hooligan . . .?

INT   CLOSE SHOT   CIAVELLI HALLWAY   NIGHT   LOUIS AT THE
TELEPHONE

> LOUIS
>
> I'd like to help you out, you know that, Gus—but I got
> mouths to feed, rent to pay—all that stuff . . . I'm not
> saying I can't get it, understand.—I'm saying I need it for
> my family . . . You're a scum—that's what you are, a
> low-down scum to talk to me like that.

There's a CRASH in the receiver. Louis winces away from the
sound, then slowly and thoughtfully hangs up. He sits, shivering in
the little damp hallway, looking at the telephone.

INT   MEDIUM SHOT   CIAVELLI HALLWAY AND BEDROOM   PAST
LOUIS IN THE F.G. TO MARIA ASLEEP IN BED
her long dark hair spread over the pillow. Louis dials a number.

> LOUIS
> (into phone)
> Look, Gus—I guess I can make it all right. I'll bring it
> around before noon—Right, Gus.

>   DISSOLVE TO:

INT   MEDIUM SHOT   DIX HANDLEY'S APARTMENT
Furnished fairly respectably, but suffering from weeks of neglect.
Dix is seated at a table, poring over a *Racing Form*. A half-finished
pint of bourbon sits in front of him. The BUZZER sounds in the
apartment. Dix is on his feet in a single movement. The buzzer
RINGS again. Then a woman's hushed voice says:

> DOLL
> (O.S.)
> It's me, honey.

> DIX
> Doll?

> DOLL
> (O.S.)
> Nobody else but me.

Dix presses the button to let her in, goes to the door, unlocks it, then
returns to the table, sitting with his back to the door. The clack of
Doll's high heels can be heard coming up the linoleum, metal-
stripped staircase.

MEDIUM SHOT   PAST DIX IN THE F.G. TOWARD THE DOOR
as Doll opens it. About thirty-five but trying to look much younger, she's tall, heavily made up, at once coarse and pretty. She wears a long cheap evening dress, half concealed by a cloth coat. She carries a small overnight bag.

> DOLL
> Sorry to brother you, honey. But—

> DIX
> Come in. Close the door.

Doll obeys. She puts the bag down, slips off her coat and throws it on a nearby chair. Leaning against the closed door, she fumbles in her handbag, finds a ragged cigarette, then scrabbles through the bag again to look for matches. Dix turns to look at her, then gets up, striking a kitchen match with his thumbnail.

MEDIUM CLOSE TWO-SHOT   DOLL AND DIX
As he holds out the flame, she looks at him, but under his hard, unsympathetic gaze, she lowers her eyes again.

> DIX
> If you're going to smoke, you got to learn to carry matches.

Doll suddenly bursts into tears. Bending down, she puts her hands over her face, then takes the broken cigarette out of her mouth and sobs convulsively. Her plump shoulders shake until she can control herself.

> DIX
> Doll—what are you crying about?

> DOLL
> Nothing, Dix—nothing, I'm sorry!

CLOSE SHOT   DIX   LOOKING AT HER

CLOSE SHOT   DOLL   WATCHING HIM
Seeing the chill, blank stare on his face, she turns away to pick up her coat.

MEDIUM SHOT
Dix doesn't help her with the coat, but goes to the window and stares out into the street.

DOLL

I'm sorry, Dix. I don't know what I was thinking about, bothering you at this time of night. I'll run along.

DIX
(his back toward her)
Gus told me the Club Royal got knocked over.

DOLL
(responding to the hint of sympathy in his voice)
Yes. Can you imagine—raiding the Royal. The cops have all gone crazy. So it's a clip joint. So what? And it had to happen on pay night!

DIX
(with an effort)
Sit down and have a drink.
Doll sits down quickly—afraid he'll change his mind.

DOLL
Don't care if I do.
She laughs as if she didn't have a care in the world. He pours her a drink.

DIX
(looking at overnight bag)
Were you locked out of your room?

DOLL
How did you guess?
Dix indicates her overnight bag. She laughs.

DOLL
(raising her glass)
Here's mud in your eye!
(then nervously)
Dix, honey, if it won't bother you too much, could I stay here a couple a days? Just a day or two.
Dix picks up a *Racing Form*, and begins studying it. Doll watches him. She thinks she has been refused. She puts her drink down and looks away from him.

A Screenplay 27

DIX
    (finally)
All right, stay if you want to—but don't you go getting any
ideas, Doll.

                                                   DISSOLVE TO:

INT CARD ROOM EMMERICH'S COUNTRY HOUSE NIGHT
A cheerful fire is burning in the fireplace. Doc is holding up an
envelope for Emmerich to see. The latter is a big man in his fifties,
with broad shoulders and a deep chest. He is wearing a well-
tailored dinner jacket. He looks, talks, and breathes affluence.
Cobby sits beaming at whoever happens to be speaking. The
inevitable drink is in his hand.

DOC
Everything is here—from the observed routine of the personnel to the alarm system—the type of locks on the doors,
and the age and condition of the main safe. Take my word
for it, Mr. Emmerich, this is a ripe plum ready to fall.

EMMERICH
My friend, according to the boys all takes are easy, but I've
made a lot of money getting them out of jail.

DOC
Please, Mr. Emmerich. Perhaps you know my reputation.
I've engineered some very big things.

COBBY
That's a fact, Mr. Emmerich. Doc here is tops.

EMMERICH
    (pointing to envelope in Doc's hand)
Am I to understand that you gathered all that information
before your last stretch?

DOC
    (nods)
That is correct. I was ready to begin operations when the
coppers grabbed me for a caper I'd almost forgotten about.

COBBY
The Adelphia Finance caper. Took them for one-
hundred-and-sixty-thousand . . . Didn't you, Doc?

DOC

Seventy.

EMMERICH

Do you really believe there's a half million in this thing?

DOC

Maybe even more.

EMMERICH

You mean that the take will be worth half a million to us in actual cash, because in no case would a fence give us more than fifty percent?

DOC

That's right, sir.

EMMERICH

What are the main problems?

DOC

There are three: money to operate—personnel—and the final disposal of the take.

COBBY

No trouble about the first, eh, Mr. Emmerich?

EMMERICH

That remains to be seen.

DOC

The helpers will be paid off like house painters. They will be told nothing about the size of the take. Sometimes men get greedy.
(he chuckles good-naturedly)

EMMERICH

How many helpers do you need?

DOC

Only three. A box man—him we pay most—maybe twenty-five thousand dollars.

COBBY

I got a guy for you—Louis Ciavelli—best peter man west of Chicago. Expert mechanic—been on some very big capers. The way I hear—he can open a safe like the back of a watch. Only he costs.

                          DOC
Then we need a top-notch driver in case of a rumble. He
should get ten thousand.
Emmerich nods.

                          DOC
And finally—sad to say—we need a hooligan. Most of
these fellows are drug addicts. They're a no-good lot or
they wouldn't be hooligans. Violence is all they know. But
they are, unfortunately, necessary. For a more or less
reliable man, I'd say—fifteen thousand.

                       EMMERICH
That's fifty thousand in all.
Doc nods. Emmerich throws his cigar in the fireplace, and taking
out his handkerchief, rubs his palms.

                       EMMERICH
How's the take to be handled?

                          DOC
We shall get in touch with the best fences in the Midwest,
and deal with the highest offer. Maybe no one fence can
handle the whole thing—in that case, we deal with two or
three.
Emmerich rises and walks back and forth across the room.

                       EMMERICH
                  (taking a deep breath)
Perhaps I . . . I'm just thinking . . . I mean, if I decide to
come into this. I, myself might handle . . .
Cobby and Doc stare at the lawyer in astonishment.

                        COBBY
You—a fence, Mr. Emmerich?

                       EMMERICH
                      (quickly)
Not exactly that, but . . . well . . . the proposition sounds
good, and I would like to see the most made of it. Every
man should stick to his own trade, I suppose, but . . .
                  (his tone becomes bolder)
I know some very big men who might not be averse to a
deal like this if properly approached—very respectable
men, I might add. Let me see what I can do before you try

to find a fence. A few days won't make any difference to
you, I imagine . . .

                    DOC
Not all all.
          (he bows deprecatingly, and spreads his hands in a
          gesture of appealing sadness)
Except for one thing, Mr. Emmerich. I dislike to mention
it, but I've just come from prison and . . .

                  EMMERICH
          (laughing good-naturedly)
Cobby here, will advance you anything you need—find
you a place to stay.—Right, Cobby?

                   COBBY
You bet your life—I got some fancy phone numbers for
you, too, Doc.
Emmerich rises. It's a signal—Doc and Cobby do likewise—
dismissed.

                  EMMERICH
          (to Doc)
What's it like—a man of your tastes—spending seven
years behind the walls?

CAMERA PULLS AHEAD as the three men go to the door.

                    DOC
Not too bad—it's a matter of temperament. I cause no
trouble. The prison authorities appreciate that. They
made me assistant librarian.

                  EMMERICH
I'm afraid I wouldn't make a model prisoner.

                    DOC
After this job, it's Mexico for me. I'll live like a king.
Mexican girls are very pretty. I'll have nothing to do all day
long, but chase them—in the sunlight.
          (turning to Emmerich)
You've been very kind, sir.
He makes an elaborate bow. Emmerich shakes hands with them,
and shows them to the door.

CLOSES THE DOOR
As the CAMERA MOVES behind Emmerich, he turns through the hall, and crosses the living room. He stops, looking down toward the couch. The CAMERA CONTINUES TO MOVE past him, to the object of his attention: Angela. We SEE her clearly for the first time. She is lying asleep, in the twisted posture, one hand entangled in her hair, an open movie magazine on the floor beside her. She is eighteen or nineteen, with a child's face and a figure that is voluptuous, if not particularly good.

MEDIUM TWO-SHOT   PAST ANGELA'S SLEEPING FACE, TOWARD EMMERICH
standing and staring at her. It is quiet in the house—quiet enough to hear the roadster pull out of the gravel driveway outside. Angela opens her eyes slowly, then twists back to look at him.

ANGELA

What's the big idea—standing there staring at me, Uncle Lon?

EMMERICH
Don't call me Uncle Lon.

ANGELA
Uncle Lon?—I thought you liked it.

EMMERICH
Maybe I did. I don't any more.

Angela sits up, a little disturbed, as Emmerich moves away from her to the big easy chair, and sitting on one of the broad arms, begins to loosen his tie.

EMMERICH
Why don't you go to bed, baby?

MEDIUM TWO-SHOT   PAST EMMERICH TO ANGELA
as she gets up, comes toward him to unbutton his collar and take off his tie.

ANGELA
Here! Let me do that.

Emmerich, a cigar between his fingers, stoops a little to lift her face with both hands.

EMMERICH
Some sweet kid!

But she escapes his caress, smiling angelically. This mixture of desire and contempt leaves her profoundly puzzled.

ANGELA
I had the market send over some salt mackerel for you—best grade they could find. I know how you love it for breakfast.

EMMERICH
(with effort)
Thanks, baby.

Angela crosses the room, turning to blow a kiss, then going into her bedroom.

ANGELA
And I love you.

EMMERICH
Sure, baby.

Emmerich watches the door shut and softly locked. Then he turns to lift a telephone from a confusion of half empty dishes and glasses on a nearby table.

MEDIUM CLOSE SHOT   EMMERICH
He dials each number with an effort, but when the connection is made, his voice takes on some of his customary hardness and vivacity.

EMMERICH
Bob Brannom? This is Emmerich.
The voice at the other end is audible, but not intelligible.

EMMERICH
(sharply)
I didn't call you to ask what time it is,—I got a job for you.
A pause—as Brannom's voice makes some distasteful comment, which reflects itself on Emmerich's face.

EMMERICH
No—nothing like that. I've got over a hundred thousand dollars on my books. Come to my office first thing in the morning.—I'll give you a list of my debtors.
Another pause.

EMMERICH
Use the methods called for in each individual case!—And don't tell me about it—all I want is results.—I need the money, I need it now, and I need it in cash. Is that clear enough?—Goodnight, Bob.

MEDIUM CLOSE SHOT
CAMERA FOLLOWS Emmerich as he walks, lighting his cigar, back toward the big easy chair. Angela's delicate, excessively high-heeled shoes are still resting on the seat. Emmerich picks them up and lets them drop wearily on the floor. He sits down in the chair and smooths his face with both hands.

EMMERICH
My God!—I'm tired.
FADE OUT:

FADE IN:

MEDIUM CLOSE SHOT DIX'S FLAT DAY DIX LYING IN BED,
ASLEEP, BUT RESTLESS AND DREAMING
An edge of sunlight cuts across his face. He is talking in his sleep,
commands, encouragement, but the words are muffled. A phone
RINGS in the apartment. CAMERA PULLS BACK into a FULL
SHOT OF THE ROOM. Doll, still in her cheap, glittering evening
dress, is washing an accumulation of dishes. She wipes her hands
and answers the phone.

DOLL

(into the phone)

Hello.—Who?—Sure, Gus . . .
She approaches the sleeping Dix, the phone in her hands, looking
down at him as he mutters in his sleep.

DOLL

(into phone)

He's still asleep . . . How's that? . . . All right, I'll tell him.
Dix opens his eyes as she hangs up. He stares at her out of his
dream.

DOLL

Honey, it was Gus. He says you can come over any time.
He's got something for you.

DIX

(smiles)

Okay.

(he gets a cigarette, lights it with satisfaction)

DOLL

Coffee, honey? I've made fresh.
Dix gets out of bed to dress. Doll pours coffee into two cups.

MEDIUM CLOSE SHOT   DOLL

DOLL

You were sure dreaming.

DIX

(O.S.)

Yeah. How do you know?

DOLL
You were talking in your sleep.

DIX
(O.S.)
What'd I say?

DOLL
It was all jumbled up, but I heard one word plain. You called it out several times—"Corn Cracker"—What's that mean?

CLOSE SHOT DIX
He pauses in his dressing.

DIX
(somberly)
Corn Cracker was a colt.

DOLL
It would be.

DIX
He was a tall, black colt. Yeah, I remember what I was dreaming. I was on that colt's back. My father and my grandfather were there—watching the fun. The colt was buck-jumpin' and pitchin'—and once he tried to scrape me off against the tree, but I stayed with him, you bet. Then I heard my grandpa say, 'He's a real Handley, that boy—a real Handley.'—And I felt proud as you please.

DOLL
Did something like that happen, Dix—when you were a kid?

DIX
Not exactly. The black colt pitched me into a fence on the first buck, and my father come over and prodded me with his boot, and said, 'Maybe that'll teach you not to brag about how good you are on a horse.'
(Dix laughs with pleasure at the recollection)

DOLL
It's nice to hear you laugh.

DIX

You know something? One of my ancestors imported the first Irish thoroughbred into our county.

DOLL
(feigning interest)
Is that a fact?

DIX

Sure . . . Our farm was in the family for generations. One hundred sixty acres—thirty in blue grass—the rest in crops—fine barn—seven broodmares.

DOLL
Sounds wonderful, Dix.

DIX

It was. Then everything happened at once—my old man died—we lost our corn crop—the black colt I was telling you about, broke his leg and had to be shot. That was a rotten year. The mares were sold to save the farm, but we lost it anyway. I'll never forget the day we left. Me and my brother swore we'd buy the farm back some day.

DOLL

Growing up on a place, and then have to leave must be awful. I never had a proper home . . . .

DIX
(heedlessly)
Twelve grand would have swung it, and I almost made it once. I had more than five thousand dollars in my pocket—Whirlaway was running in the Preakness. I figured he couldn't lose. I put it all on his nose. He lost by a nose.

DOLL
Drink your coffee, honey, before it gets cold.
He raises the cup to his lips.

DIX

The way I figure, my luck's just got to turn . . . One of these days, I'll make a real killing. Then I'll hit for home. First thing I do when I get there, is take a bath in the creek and get the city dirt off me.

Doll says nothing. Her lower lip is quivering. She is swallowing
hard. Dix's gaze finally settles on her.

                              DIX
                    What's the matter?
                         (she shakes her head)
                    Did I say something wrong?

                              DOLL
                    No, honey, no.
                         (she looks around the room)
                    Gee this place's a mess—needs a good cleaning. How can
                    you stand to live like this?
Dix looks at her, his thoughts elsewhere.

                                              DISSOLVE TO:

INT MEDIUM SHOT COBBY'S OFFICE DAY
Dix is standing opposite Cobby, who has placed the barrier of a
desk between them. On the desk lies a thick roll of bills, bound up
in an elastic band.

                              DIX
Count it.

                            COBBY
                   (nervous and uneasy)
Look, Dix, you don't have to pay the whole tab at once.

                              DIX
                        (sullenly)
Count it.
Cobby obeys, thumbing through the roll as hastily as he can.

                            COBBY
                      (as he counts)
Why get sore? No reason to get sore.

                              DIX
You boned me in front of a stranger. Trying to make me
look small.

                            COBBY
                   (pocketing the money)
I tell you, I didn't mean it. I shoot my mouth off. Maybe I
had a slight load on. You know how it is.

                              DIX
I don't know how it is.

                            COBBY
Listen, Dix. I made a mistake. Don't you ever make a
mistake?

MEDIUM CLOSE SHOT   DIX
He rubs his hand slowly over his face. Paying off the debt to Cobby
has not turned out to be the satisfaction he expected.

                            COBBY
                         (O.S.)
Here—how about a drink? I got a bottle of Scotch laid
away—best you can buy. I keep it for my very best friends.

                              DIX
                   (with some contempt)
I don't drink Scotch. Got some bourbon in the joint?

COBBY
(O.S.)
Sure, sure.

MEDIUM CLOSE   COBBY
as he fixes Dix a drink.

COBBY
You know, Dix. You got to play the horses the smart way.
Save your money—next time there's a fix going—I'll let
you know. It'll be money from home, money from home.
There's a knock at the door, tentative, polite. CAMERA PANS
WITH Cobby as he opens the door. It's Doc Riedenschneider,
wearing gloves now, a better suit, his homburg blocked and
brushed.

COBBY
It's the Doc!—Come on in. Meet a friend of mine—Dix
Handley.

MEDIUM THREE-SHOT   AS THE DOC ENTERS
shaking hands first with Cobby, then with Dix. They eye one
another with respect.

COBBY
This is Doc Riedenschneider, Dix. You've heard of him, I
guess.

DIX
Yeah.

COBBY
Well, how do you like that whiskey? Made in your home
state.

DOC
(to Dix)
Oh!—Where's that, sir?

DIX
Kentucky. Boone County, Kentucky.
He takes off his hat. Without it, he is surprisingly relaxed and
human once more.

DIX

It's the water. Best water in the U.S.A.

DOC

Is that so?

DIX

(still to Doc)

It's the water makes whiskey fit to drink.

Dix has finished his drink. Now he picks up his hat and goes to the door.

DIX

Well, I got to go. See you around, maybe.

And he leaves. Cobby shuts the door.

COBBY

(sighs with relief)

That big hick . . . The color of his money's all right . . . but I wish he wasn't so touchy.

DOC

Maybe it's a point of honor with him . . . a gambling debt.

COBBY

Him—that hooligan! Honor! Don't make me laugh!

DOC

He's a hooligan, you say?

COBBY

Yeah, but a small-timer—little stick-ups—cigar stores, gas stations . . . and every cent goes to the ponies.

DOC

One way or another we all work for our vice.

COBBY

You said it. How about it, Doc, did you have a good time last night?

DOC

The young lady drank too much to be good company. But the evening wasn't a complete loss. She talked more than if she'd been sober.

                    COBBY
Yeah? What about?

                    DOC
Your friend Mr. Emmerich.

                    COBBY
Emmerich! Now, look here, Doc—!

                    DOC
        (gravely)
There's a half a million at stake. I've got to know where I
stand. Emmerich must put up before I can hire a crew.

                    COBBY
For him, that's nothing! A dead cinch!

                    DOC
The information she gave me is that he's broke.

                    COBBY
Are you crazy?—Look, I've seen Mr. Emmerich operate
for twenty years—he handles only the biggest cases. He's
got two houses, four cars, half a dozen servants . . .

                    DOC
And one redhead?

                    COBBY
Doc, whose word will you take—mine or some dim-
witted dame's?

                    DOC
        (politely)
Yours, naturally . . .

                    COBBY
Well, if he's broke, I want to be broke the same way.

Suddenly the office door opens. Lietuenant Ditrich takes a step into
the room. He's in plainclothes—and alone. He stands staring at Doc
as if he were seeing a ghost. For a long moment, everyone is frozen.

CLOSE SHOT   DITRICH
as he abruptly turns back into the corridor.

CLOSE SHOT   COBBY
slowly rising from his seat.

CLOSE SHOT   DOC

INT MEDIUM SHOT DAY THE CORRIDOR OUTSIDE COBBY'S
OFFICE
Lieutenant Ditrich walks toward the outside door, his back to
Cobby, who emerges from his office, running after him. CAMERA
FOLLOWS.

CAMERA MOVES INTO A CLOSER TWO-SHOT OF COBBY AND
DITRICH

> COBBY
>
> That guy in my office—He's just passing through,
> Lieutenant.

> DITRICH
>
> Shut up—I didn't see anybody—How could I? I wasn't
> there.

> COBBY
>   (grinning)
> Yeah—that's right . . .

> DITRICH
>   (frowning)
> Look—I just came to tell you: You'll have to stand still for a
> raid.

> COBBY
>
> You mean you have to haul me downtown and book me?

> DITRICH
>
> It's a short ride.

> COBBY
>
> I thought you were a friend of mine—

> DITRICH
>
> Right now, I've got one friend—
>   (points to himself)
> —Ditrich. And Ditrich's going to be out on his ear if he
> don't make a showing.

COBBY

All right, but why me? Why pick on me?

DITRICH

Because it's logic. You're the biggest parlor in my precinct, and citizens know it, and the newspapers know it, and even I know it. And that little Commissioner knows I know it.

COBBY

I hate to have it happen. I just hate it, that's all.

DITRICH

I'm as sorry as you are.

He is let out by a worried, mute Timmons. Cobby pushes out of the doorway to hold him by the sleeve.

COBBY

Look, Lieutenant—I've always given you plenty cooperation. But you're hitting me just the wrong time.

DITRICH

(deliberates, then)

All right. But close up. Tight. Keep the place dark. Don't answer phones.

COBBY

Thanks, Lieutenant.—I'll show you my appreciation.

Ditrich leaves Cobby standing in the doorway. CAMERA MOVES BACK as Cobby darts down the corridor again.

CUT TO:

INT   COBBY'S OFFICE

as the little man bounces in.

DOC

(lighting a cigar)

That copper—he recognized me.

COBBY

How'd you know he was a copper?

DOC

I can smell one a block off.

COBBY

Now don't worry about Ditrich. He's on my payroll—
practically a partner. Me and him we're just like that!
He holds up two fingers.

DOC

Experience has taught me never to trust a policeman. Just
when you think one's all right he turns legit on you.

DISSOLVE TO:

INT   ENTRANCE HALL   EMMERICH'S HOUSE   NIGHT
The floor is checkered marble. A large crystal chandelier illuminates
the stair which rises to a balcony overhanging the entrance. O.S.
the sound of knocking. A butler appears on the balcony and descends the stairs, opens the front door. Brannom, a tough-looking,
flashily dressed man in his early thirties stands there.

BRANNOM

Mr. Emmerich at home?

EVANS
(disapproval in his voice)
Who shall I say is calling?

BRANNOM

Mr. Brannom.

EVANS

Wait here, please.
He leaves Brannom standing in the middle of the hall. CAMERA
DOLLIES WITH Evans through the living room to the study. He
raps on the study door.

EMMERICH'S VOICE
(O.S.)
Come in.
Evans opens the door. Emmerich is seated at a desk, writing checks.

EVANS

A Mr. Brannom is here.

EMMERICH

Show him in, please.

EVANS
Pardon me, sir, but Mrs. Emmerich is not feeling well.

EMMERICH
Send for Dr. Housman.

EVANS
I already have, sir.

EMMERICH
Good. I'll be up to see her later.

Evans leaves the room. Emmerich walks back and forth across the
study until his guest appears. Brannom's dark face has a sad, tough
look. Emmerich closes the study door, motions him to a chair.

EMMERICH
(cheerfully)
Well? How about my debtors?

He shifts uneasily, trying to hide his nervousness.

EMMERICH
How many came through?

BRANNOM
Not a one.

EMMERICH
(cries)
What's that?

BRANNOM
Want all the excuses? I've got some beauts.

EMMERICH
(sitting down heavily)
That bad, eh?

BRANNOM
Two or three may come through with a part. They promised.

EMMERICH
I don't want promises—I want cash!

BRANNOM

Look, my friend, I'm a licensed private eye. I can't go
around threatening these people—especially in your
name. Ninety-eight percent of them you're going to have
to sue.

EMMERICH
(abruptly)
Takes too long. I need money now—this minute.

BRANNOM
What is it—girl trouble?

He laughs coarsely. The sound of his laughter enrages Emmerich.

EMMERICH
Shut up, Brannom—this isn't funny!

BRANNOM
(quietly but harshly)
How's that?
(he pales slightly, and sits forward in his chair)
Nobody tells me to shut up . . .

Emmerich glances up; sees the look in Brannom's narrowed eyes;
realizes he has gone too far.

EMMERICH
I'm sorry, Bob.
(suddenly he breaks down)
It's all a gag . . . a silly, sad, trumped-upped gag!

He puts his head in his hands, and sits huddled over, shaken by dry
sobs. Brannom shows astonishment at first, then his eyes grow
wise and his lip curls in contempt.

BRANNOM
If it's that redhead, my friend—no dame's worth it.

The sobs continue. Brannom goes to the whiskey; pours a stiff slug.
He turns to Emmerich, and thrusts the drink into his hands.

BRANNOM
Here!

Emmerich glances up, sees the contempt in Brannom's eyes;
finishes the drink with one swallow; then, closing his eyes, he
begins to speak.

EMMERICH
I'm broke, Bob. That's the plain, simple fact. Finished.
Bankrupt.

BRANNOM
I don't believe you.

EMMERICH
It's true. I can't believe it myself, but it's true. Sure, I get
big fees, but they're spent before they're collected.

BRANNOM
(gesturing to indicate the ornate room)
What about all this?

EMMERICH
Mortgaged—
(indicating his neck)
—up to here . . .

BRANNOM
How could you let a dame like Angela take you this way?

EMMERICH
It's not only Angela—it's everything—my whole style of
life. See that piece?
(he points to a Chippendale desk)
It cost eight thousand dollars. I detest it!—as I do everything else about this absurd house—including the whining woman upstairs who pretends to be sick in order to
hold me. I should have got rid of this house and her too.
But I didn't have the courage. So what do I do but take on a
stupid, mercenary dame, and I put her up in another
absurd house. Ten thousand here—ten thousand there—
I've got to get out from under. And the irony of it is I have
the opportunity . . . and can't take it.

BRANNOM
Tough.

EMMERICH
Bob, I'm going to give you the shock of your life . . .
You've heard of Doc Riedenschneider?

BRANNOM
Sure. Behind the Walls, isn't he?

EMMERICH
He got out a week ago. Cobby brought him around. He
has a plan, beautifully worked out, for the biggest caper
ever to be pulled in the Midwest. He wants fifty thousand
dollars backing.

BRANNOM
Who'd be taken?

EMMERICH
Belletier's.
(Brannom whistles)
The rocks alone should bring—conservatively speak-
ing—half a million.

BRANNOM
How much would you get out of it?

EMMERICH
One third of the take . . .

BRANNOM
Brother, you're knocking me out!

EMMERICH
What if I said I'd figured out a way of getting it all?
Brannom elevates his eyebrows.

EMMERICH
I could tell him I, myself, would fence the stuff—Promise
him cash on delivery.—But, when the time came, I
wouldn't have the cash. I could tell him it would take
another day or two, and I'm certain I could get him to leave
the stuff with me while waiting.

BRANNOM
(hoarsely)
Go on.

EMMERICH
(shrugs)
Then I could disappear. Take a plane to another coun-

try—to another life.—Melt down the gold and platinum
and sell it as bullion.—Dispose of the rocks one by one.
There'd be no hurry.—They'd last a lifetime.

                    BRANNOM
          (laughs a coarse, sudden laugh)
How wrong can a guy be? Here I was—worrying about
your nerves and you were dreaming up a double-cross
like this.

                    EMMERICH
But I can't do it for want of fifty thousand dollars.

                    BRANNOM
I can tell you how to raise it.

                    EMMERICH
How?

                    BRANNOM
What's in it for me?

                    EMMERICH
Half of the rocks.

                    BRANNOM
Okay. But we may get ourselves killed, my friend.

                    EMMERICH
I know.
Brannom laughs again.

                    EMMERICH
How do we raise the dough?

                    BRANNOM
Simple. We take Cobby in.

                    EMMERICH
          (incredulously)
Cobby?

                    BRANNOM
Believe me. He can dig it up without half trying.

                    EMMERICH
But what do we tell him? Why do I need it?

BRANNOM

Leave it to me. Cobby wants to feel big. Here's his chance.
Advancing money for the great Alonzo P. Emmerich. Oh,
he'll do it.
            (lifting his glass)
He'll sweat, but he'll do it.

DISSOLVE TO:

FULL SHOT   COBBY'S "BOILER ROOM"

The place has been closed. The telephones ring at intervals during
the next scene, but no one answers them. Talking at an empty desk
are Doc and Louis Ciavelli. Doc has several papers which he has
taken out of an old envelope. Louis is studying them. Cobby sits a
little apart at another empty desk on which a metal box is sitting.

DOC

What boxes have you opened?

LOUIS

Cannon Ball, Diebold, Double Door—even a few fire
chests,—all of 'em.

DOC

Can you open a Diebold with a time lock and relocking
device?

LOUIS

Sure.

DOC

What do you use, lock or seam?

LOUIS

Seam.

DOC

Ever taken one?

LOUIS

Remember the Shafter job?

DOC

Yes, I heard about it behind the Walls. It was a good score.
Who supplies your soup?

LOUIS
I thrash it myself.

DOC
How are you as a pick lock?

LOUIS
I can open any lock in four minutes.

DOC
You'll do. You're in.

LOUIS
That depends. What's the cut?

DOC
No cut. You get a flat guarantee.

LOUIS
(considers, then)
I want thirty thousand.

COBBY
Thirty thousand!—Now, Louis.

DOC
Twenty-five thousand is what we figured.

LOUIS
All right. Fifteen down.

COBBY
Ten down.

DOC
Fifteen is satisfactory, I think.
(turning to Cobby)
There's your paymaster.

CLOSE TWO-SHOT   COBBY AND LOUIS
Cobby opens the steel box, pays out the fifteen thousand to
Louis.—It hurts him to pay out money.

LOUIS
What are you sweating for?

COBBY
Money makes me sweat, that's all. That's the way I am.

CLOSE SHOT   DOC WATCHING COBBY

MEDIUM SHOT   DOC, COBBY, LOUIS
as Cobby pays out.

LOUIS
(pocketing the wads of money)
Who are the others on this job, Doc?

DOC
Haven't got 'em yet.

LOUIS
There's only one driver, far as I'm concerned. His name is
Gus Minissi. Ask Cobby—he knows him.

COBBY
Gus? He's hundred percent. He'll take all the heat and he
won't flap his lip.

DOC
Get hold of him.

COBBY
Sure, Doc.

DOC
Any ideas about a hooligan?
Louis frowns, puzzling over the problem.

COBBY
I know a very tough heavy, but I haven't see him for some
time. Red Traynor.

LOUIS
He's taking the cure.

DOC
Rule him out.

COBBY
What about Timmons?

DOC
Who's that?

COBBY

My doorman.

LOUIS

That busted-down wrestler? You must be kidding. He's
got nothing up here but solid knuckle.

DOC
(softly and mildly)
I'm a stranger, and do not know as much as you gentlemen, but what about this southerner? This Dix?

MEDIUM CLOSE TWO-SHOT   LOUIS AND COBBY
They exchange glances.

MEDIUM CLOSE SHOT   THE DOC
He looks at each of them in turn, studying them. He speaks deliber-
ately.

DOC
He impressed me as a very determined man and far from
stupid.

MEDIUM SHOT   ALL THREE MEN   COBBY, LOUIS, DOC

LOUIS

Frankly, I don't like the guy. But I never saw a hooligan I
did like. They're like left-handed pitchers, all with a screw
loose.
Suddenly there's a silence. They've come to an impasse.

LOUIS
(remembering)
Probably be as good as anybody, thought. Gus thinks he's
tops. And Gus is usually right.

DOC

I like him. I say we take him.

LOUIS
(going out)
Suits me. You're the boss.

LOUIS
(all the money in his pockets)
Well, I got to be getting home. Maria—that's **my wife**—
she's worried about the kid.

DOC
(politely)
What's the trouble?

LOUIS
Oh, he's got a cold again. She takes him out first thing in the morning. I tell her, it's too cold. But she claims, a baby's got to taste the fresh air. I say to her, if you want fresh air, don't look for it in this town. Well—always problems—

DOC
I must say I envy you—being a family man.

He goes out. CAMERA MOVES INTO A MEDIUM CLOSE TWO-SHOT OF DOC AND COBBY.

COBBY
One good thing about Dix Handley. You can get him for nickels and dimes.

DOC
Tell me something, Cobby. That's your money, isn't it—not Mr. Emmerich's?

COBBY
What difference does it make?

DOC
None really.

COBBY
It's this way—Mr. Emmerich didn't want this transaction appearing on his books. Oh, I'm not risking anything—he's good for it in case of a run-out.

DOC
Then you haven't got a worry.

DISSOLVE TO:

MEDIUM SHOT   DIX'S APARTMENT
No longer is it a litter of dirty dishes, cigarette ends and old *Racing Forms*. Doll has made it spic and span. Dix stands by the window looking out. The curtains are clean and the panes sparkle. O.S. Doll's step. Dix turns.

CLOSE SHOT   DOLL PAST DIX
She is wearing a hat and is carrying a little valise.

                         DIX
         Where are you going?

                         DOLL
         I found a place.
Dix is a little startled, but shows a blank face.

                         DIX
         Did you?

                         DOLL
              (nods)
         Yeah. A girl friend of mine is leaving town and she's
         letting me have her apartment. It's all paid up 'til the first
         of next month.

                         DIX
         When did this all happen?

                         DOLL
         This morning before you woke up. I bumped into her on
         the street. Remember that tall brunette who did novelty
         dances at the Band Wagon—Blanche La Rue? It was sure
         nice of her—and—I can't go on living off you forever, can
         I?
She is extremely nervous; emotionally unstrung; maybe on the
verge of breaking down. Dix shifts his eyes downward to the floor.

                         DIX
              (his voice unnaturally polite)
         I was glad to help out.

                         DOLL
         Maybe I can do something for you some time.

                         DIX
         You don't owe me a thing—forget it.

                         DOLL
         Well—goodbye.

DIX
(uneasily)
How you fixed for dough?

DOLL
A few bucks—enough.

Dix fumbles in his pants pocket and comes up with a twenty-dollar
bill.

DIX
Here—and if things don't work out . . . .

DOLL
No, Dix—thanks—and I'm all through bothering you.
Give us a kiss.

He puts his arms around her rather awkwardly—Doll relaxes in
them. But it is a brief kiss. Doll picks up her bag and goes to the
door. She is starting down the stairs when Dix calls to her.

DIX
Doll!

CUT TO:

CLOSE SHOT   DOLL ON THE STAIR
She turns; a look of hope in her eyes. CAMERA PANS WITH HER
TO:

CLOSE TWO-SHOT   DOLL AND DIX

DOLL
Yes, Dix?

DIX
(after a pause; almost angrily)
Maybe I'll want to get in touch with you.

DOLL
(in a small voice)
Oh yes—my new address—I'll be at 42 Merton Street.

DIX
. . . 42 Merton Street.

She turns quickly; goes down the stairs. THE CAMERA FOLLOWS
Dix into his apartment. He goes to the table; sits down; picks up the
Racing Form. It's no use, he can't concentrate. He puts it down, folds

his big hands, and looks into space. He remains there for some time—thinking unhappily. Then the phone RINGS.

> DIX
> (picking up the phone)
> Hello. Oh, hello, Cobby . . . Yeah . . . .

He continues to listen.

DISSOLVE TO:

INT MEDIUM SHOT GUS'S HAMBURGER STAND NIGHT
A dark storeroom, lit with a single bulb. Seated on boxes of canned goods are the whole crew: Doc, Louis, Dix and Gus.

MEDIUM SHOT ALL FOUR MEN: DOC, LOUIS, DIX, GUS

> DOC
> Here's everything. The soft spot's an old steam tunnel. Manhole's on the corner. Break through here.
> (he points to map)
> It'll take you about six minutes to get into Belletier's through their furnace room. Watch out for floor wires,

make your way up to the back door and jump the alarm circuit. That'll take you another three minutes. Dix will cover you. At exactly eleven-fifty-four we go to the back door. You open it for us.

                    LOUIS
I'll be ready.

                    DOC
We should be through with our business not later than twelve-fifteen. The movie lets out at twelve-twenty. We'll move away with the crowd. Louis will drive back by himself. Dix will come with Gus and me and the jewelry. Any questions?

                    LOUIS
Everything sounds okay.

                    GUS
Same here.

                    LOUIS
        (getting up)
I'll be getting on home.

                    DOC
How's the boy?

                    LOUIS
Oh, he's okay. Ran a temperature yesterday—pretty high. We called the doctor, but temperatures don't mean anything much with kids. He's normal today.
        (to Dix)
See you tomorrow night—eleven-thirty.

Gus goes with Louis to let him out the front door. Dix finds his hat, puts it on, starts to rise.

MEDIUM CLOSE TWO-SHOT   DOC AND DIX

                    DOC
Have you got a minute, Dix?

                    DIX
        (sitting back)
Sure. What's on your mind?

DOC

My friend, what do you know about this fellow Emmerich?

DIX

You mean the Big Fixer?
(Doc nods)
I've heard his name—that's all.

DOC
(smiles, ingratiatingly)
I can talk to you, I think.

DIX

Sure.

DOC

Mr. Emmerich is taking the jewelry off our hands.

DIX

You sure are surprising me, Doc.

DOC

I don't exactly trust Mr. Emmerich. It's just a feeling—I may be wrong, but it's up to us to collect—you and me. Everything may go smooth, but if it don't . . .

DIX
(shortly)
If he's got it—we'll collect.

DOC

Good. We will meet Mr. Emmerich after the caper— deliver the jewelry, and get our money. The payment is to be immediate and in cash. After that we will pay off and scatter.

DIX
(nodding)
Don't worry, Doc—we'll collect—

DISSOLVE TO:

INSERT   PLANE TICKET   PASSPORT   WALLET CLOCK ON DRESSER TOP
The clock says 11:25. In the mirror we SEE Emmerich close a travel-

ing case. He comes toward dresser, his hand picks up the ticket, etc.
CAMERA PULLS BACK THEN DOLLIES WITH HIM as he carries
his case out into the hall . . . A bedroom door is ajar; as he is about
to pass a woman's voice calls, "Lon." Emmerich puts the case
down, opens the door.

FULL SHOT   MRS. EMMERICH'S BEDROOM
Originally furnished in rather soft, gentle and feminine good taste,
there has been superimposed upon it the metal furnishings of a
chronic invalid: three therapeutic lamps, a special reading light
with a bluish daylight bulb, which throws a ghastly glow over the
bed and two night tables loaded with bottles, glass eyecups,
spoons, scattered cards, and a pile of magazines. Mrs. Emmerich is
sitting up in bed in a food-stained bed jacket.

                    MRS. EMMERICH
          Lon!

                    EMMERICH
               (at the door)
          Yes, May . . . ?

                    MRS. EMMERICH
          Come in, Lon . . . Sit down a minute.
Emmerich enters, sits down. She folds a corner of the page in her
magazine; takes off her horn-rimmed glasses.

                    EMMERICH
          I've got a business appointment . . . .

                    MRS. EMMERICH
          It's almost eleven thirty. Isn't that rather late for—
          business.
               (Emmerich chooses to ignore her remark)
          Lon—

                    EMMERICH
          Yes, May.

                    MRS. EMMERICH
          I'm not feeling well.

                    EMMERICH
               (not unkindly)
          You haven't been feeling well for a long time.

MEDIUM TWO-SHOT EMMERICH IN THE F.G. TOWARD MRS.
EMMERICH
as she moves restlessly under the chafing covers.

> MRS. EMMERICH
> At night I get nervous, and when I get nervous I hate to
> stay in this big house all my myself.

> EMMERICH
> But May—you're not alone. There are three servants in
> this house, and all you have to do is—

> MRS. EMMERICH
> I know—press a button.—Did it ever occur to you that I
> might want something that couldn't be brought to me by a
> servant on a tray.

Emmerich gets out of the chair and begins to walk up and down in
his wife's room.

> EMMERICH
> Do you want me to sit here and watch you read a maga-
> zine?

> MRS. EMMERICH
> Would that be so awful?

MEDIUM CLOSE SHOT EMMERICH
as he pauses beside his wife's bed.

> EMMERICH
> Look, May . . .

> MRS. EMMERICH
> We could play cards—cassino—like we used to.

> EMMERICH
> Some other night.

> MRS. EMMERICH
> Please, Lon.

> EMMERICH
> Look, May, this is an important appointment. I must keep
> it!

He glances at his watch.

CUT TO:

INSERT OF WATCH
It's a little before 11:30.

                    MRS. EMMERICH
          Please, Lon, just one hand . . . .
                    (she turns her face away from him)
          I couldn't sleep last night, and I got to thinking about the
          old days—how we used to like to stay up and play cas-
          sino—
                    (Emmerich hesitates. She begins shuffling an old,
                    swollen pack of cards)
          —just the two of us.

                    EMMERICH
          I can't stay. I wish I could—but I can't. This is business.
                    (he goes to the door)
          Maybe I'll look in and see you later if you're still awake.
Mrs. Emmerich nods, still shuffling her cards. Emmerich goes out.

MEDIUM SHOT   STAIRCASE IN THE EMMERICH HOUSE
As Emmerich, suitcase in hand, hurriedly descends. CAMERA
MOVES DOWN WITH HIM, including, as he opens the door to the
darkness outside, a huge grandfather clock that begins to chime the
half-hour: eleven-thirty.

                                        DISSOLVE TO:

EXT   MEDIUM SHOT   A ONE-STORY GARAGE BUILDING   NIGHT
A car drives out. Louis is at the wheel. He stops briefly at the corner.
Dix gets in.

INT   CLOSE SHOT   CAR
He drives on in silence for some time, then Louis fishes in his
pocket, takes out a pack of cigarettes, offers it to Dix. They both light
up.

                    DIX
          Where's the soup?
Louis silently shows Dix the bottle tied around his neck by a string.

                                        DISSOLVE TO:

FULL SHOT   CAR PULLING INTO AN ALLEYWAY
Gus is at the wheel. Doc steps out of a doorway. Gets in beside him.
Without a word, Gus drives on.

DISSOLVE TO:

EXT   MEDIUM LONG TRUCKING SHOT   STREET NEAR
BELLETIER'S   NIGHT
shooting through Dix and Louis through the windshield as they
turn into a parking lot, picking a space as close as possible to the
exit. As the car, and MOVING SHOT come into a stop, the long
brick wall and the marquee of a movie house are visible.

DIX

You all set?

LOUIS

Help me with my coat.

MEDIUM SHOT   PARKING LOT NEAR MOVIE   AS THE TWO MEN
GET OUT OF LOUIS'S CAR
Louis comes around the front and puts both hands into the sleeves
of the overcoat which Dix holds out for him. The coat jingles slightly
as it comes down over his shoulders. As they walk away from the
car, the CAMERA MOVES BEHIND THEM, crossing the parking lot
and around to the back alley behind Belletier's. They make their
way to the far end of the alley where they both open a manhole with
a jimmy twenty-eight inches long which Louis draws from his left
trouser leg. The manhole cover comes off. Louis silently takes Dix's
hand and deposits the soup bottle in his palm. He then unties the
string from behind his neck, leaving Dix holding the precious
bottle.

LOUIS

Watch out how you handle this or they'll pick you up in
little pieces.

Louis goes through the manhole. Dix kicks the cover back on after
Louis has disappeared. Dix then walks calmly to the corner of the
alley and takes his position as lookout.

DISSOLVE TO:

LOUIS IN THE STEAM TUNNEL
(this shot to be described according to research)

DISSOLVE TO:

DOC AND GUS
Arriving at their position. Doc looks at his watch.

INSERT   WATCH
The time is eleven-forty-eight.

DISSOLVE TO:

LOUIS IN THE STEAM TUNNEL
(this shot to be described according to research)

DISSOLVE TO:

DIX
Patrolling slowly between the manhole and the corner of the alley.

DISSOLVE TO:

LOUIS IN THE TUNNEL
(third shot to be chosen)

DISSOLVE TO:

DOC AND GUS
Doc gets out of the car and saunters to the corner. He is carrying an
old-fashioned large briefcase. Doc looks at his watch.

INSERT   WATCH
The time is eleven-fifty-four.

DOC
strolling slowly toward the alley, meets Dix at the corner. They walk slowly in the direction of the back door of Belletier's.

DOC
Did he give you the soup?
Dix, without a word, shows Doc the bottle in his hand. They arrive at the precise time as the back door opens from inside. Doc and Dix swiftly move through the opening as Louis holds up the wire which he has rigged to jump the alarm circuit. The door shuts once more, slowly and carefully, on the empty alley. Entrance has been accomplished.

CUT TO:

INT FULL SHOT BELLETIER'S SHOWROOM NIGHT
inside the showroom of Belletier's and Co. There are shadowy galleries overhead, and everywhere the dark reflection from mirrors, polished floors, metal and glass, lamps and ornaments. The showcases themselves are covered with shroudlike sheets to keep off the dust. The footsteps of the three men can be heard emerging onto the slick floor.

DOC
Follow me.
He indicates the direction and they follow into the main part of the store. They move toward the vault.

DOC
(to Louis)
There it is.
Turning to Dix, he gestures with his head indicating the front of the store. Dix hands the bottle back to Louis, then makes his way to a window. Louis puts the soup back around his neck. As Doc and Louis are about to enter the alcove in which the vault is housed:

DOC
Here's their secret alarm—the electric eye. We'll have to crawl under the beam.

CUT TO:

DIX
Arriving at his position in the front of the store. He looks out through the drawn shade and remains there.

CUT BACK TO:

INT   MEDIUM CLOSE SHOT   BELLETIER'S
Doc sits down on a customer's chair, leaning down a little to light a cigar but cupping the flame carefully.

INT   MEDIUM CLOSE SHOT   BELLETIER'S   DIX
behind a column in the store, looking out toward the Square. He opens his coat to reveal the angle of his gun held in the waistband of his trousers.

INT   MEDIUM SHOT   BELLETIER'S   THE SHEET OVER THE SCREEN BEFORE THE VAULT
A tiny point of light is visible moving behind it, casting a sharp shadow of Louis's face on the sheet for just a moment. Then the light goes out. A second later we hear the sound of a small electric motor going up to speed.

CLOSE SHOT   DOC
slowly drawing at his cigar. There is the sound of the electric tool, drilling in spurts like a dentist's drill.

CLOSE SHOT   DIX
looking past the plate glass windows of the store.

CLOSE SHOT   LOUIS
his face is calm, intent, as if he were a craftsman doing a customary but difficult job. The sound of the electric drill continues.

DISSOLVE TO:

INT   MEDIUM THREE-SHOT   BELLETIER'S SHOWROOM   NIGHT
Doc is still smoking his cigar, Dix is still quietly watching toward the street. Louis is only visible as a hand or a foot emerges from behind the screen that hides the door of the vault, as he shifts to get into a better position. The sound of the drilling continues.

> DOC
> (to Louis)
> How much longer do you need?

> LOUIS
> Almost ready.
> (after a pause)
> It's going to take a lot to blow this baby.
> (He finishes drilling. He pours the soup.)

Here goes!
There is the sound of a dull, heavy, muffled blast. Doc and Louis enter the vault. They look at the keester. Louis immediately goes to work on it with his drill. O.S. the distant sound of an alarm bell is heard. Dix comes to the opening of the vault.

DIX
Hey, Doc. Alarms are going off all over the block.

LOUIS
The blast must have shook up the circuit.

DIX
What do we do?

DOC
I would hate to leave now. We are so close.

DIX
I'm for finishing what we started.

DOC
How about you, Louis?

LOUIS

Okay by me.

DOC

Will Gus hold still?

DIX

Don't worry about Gus.

There is a sudden sharp sound of something breaking. The drill stops.

CLOSE SHOT   ON LOUIS

There are silent Italian curses mouthed by his lips.

DOC

What is it?

LOUIS

Drill broke.

There is a faint jingle of metal as Louis begins to fish in his overcoat for the extra drill.

DOC

We should finish before twelve-fifteen—before the watchman gets here.

DIX

A store cop? Let me worry about him, Doc.

DOC

I hope that will not be necessary.

A siren is heard O.S. in the distance. It grows louder and now another one begins somewhat lower in pitch. A third siren joins in.

DOC

Hear that, Dix?

DIX

Yeah . . . .

DOC

Coming this way?

DIX

From the river. Don't sound good.

A sharp banging is heard as Louis uses his hammer. The door of the keester is opened by Louis. Doc pulls open a capacious briefcase. In a pinpoint of light held in Louis's left hand, he and Doc dump the contents of tray after velvet tray into the briefcase. The loot rattles like marbles as it is thrown together. The sirens are now so loud they seem to fill the whole room and the whole neighborhood.

> DOC
> (not ceasing work for a second)
> Dix, take a look. See what's happening.

MEDIUM SHOT   BELLETIER'S SHOWROOM
as Dix works his way forward to get a look through the front windows.

> DIX
> They're working the Square. Door by door.

> DOC
> (O.S.)
> How far away?

> DIX
> Up and down the block.

> LOUIS
> (O.S.)
> That's all, Doc.

> DIX
> (his face turning into CAMERA)
> Let's blow fast.

> DOC
> Dix—take a look at the back door.

CAMERA FOLLOWS DIX as he goes swiftly back through the store, passing between Louis and Doc as they wait for him to go ahead into the rear corridor. Doc is fastening the briefcase.

> LOUIS
> (to Doc, with pride, indicating the briefcase)
> She's heavy, ain't she?

> DOC
> Plenty.
> (with a note of triumph in his voice)
> This is the biggest one yet. Wait 'til you see it in the papers.

Both men begin to move toward the rear corridor, almost pitch black, into which Dix has preceded them.

MEDIUM SHOT   INSIDE CORRIDOR AND AT REAR DOOR OF BELLETIER'S
as Dix slowly opens it, admitting a slit of light from the back alley that cuts across his face and hands. Then he stops moving, freezes. First an elongated shadow, then a man appears in the back alley, moving toward the door. He's a heavy young man in his thirties, wearing a private police uniform, and carrying a gun in a black leather holster.

EXT   MEDIUM CLOSE SHOT   NIGHT   THE BACK ALLEY
The watchman sees the inch-wide opening of the door, puts his hand on it, then pulls it back, and draws his gun. Then he advances again.

INT   MEDIUM SHOT   INSIDE THE REAR CORRIDOR   NIGHT
past Dix in the F.G., toward Louis and Doc as they come up toward him.

DIX
Watchman. Pull open the door, Louis.

LOUIS
Maybe he'll go away.

DOC
Do what Dix says.
Louis moves toward the door.

EXT   MEDIUM SHOT   ALLEY OUTSIDE BELLETIER'S   NIGHT   THE WATCHMAN
as he moves slowly, the gun in his right hand, toward the rear door. Suddenly the door is jerked inward, and Dix is revealed in the full light from the alley outside. Both men stand frozen for a fraction of a second. Then THE CAMERA MOVES IN BEHIND the watchman as Dix grabs him by the left arm, pulls him forward suddenly, and at the same time hits him full on the chin. The blow is sure and heavy, but the watchman doesn't fall, because Dix still has hold of his left sleeve. Then he lets him go, as the watchman sags forward onto the polished stone floor. CAMERA RUSHES FORWARD TOWARD HIM as he falls. His left arm strikes the floor first, then the side of his

head. The gun flies out of his right hand, strikes the stone, and there
is a flash and an echoing roar in the stone corridor—then silence.

MEDIUM THREE-SHOT   INSIDE THE REAR CORRIDOR
BELLETIER'S   PAST DOC AND DIX
in the F.G., as they look at one another in dismay. Behind them, in
the half-darkness, Louis lets go of the door, sways back as though
he were drunk, and then falls to his knees with a groan. Dix turns
and lifts him to his feet again. Louis groans again.

DIX
(to Doc)

Come on—I'll carry him.
Dix lifts Louis over his shoulder.

LOUIS

Take it easy—you're killing me.

EXT   MEDIUM LONG SHOT   THE ALLEY BACK OF BELLETIER'S
NIGHT
CAMERA PANS WITH THE THREE MEN as they leave through the
rear door across the alley, and enter the parking lot. At the further
end Gus in his car flashes the car lights on for a second.

MEDIUM LONG SHOT   TWO SIDES OF THE SQUARE ON WHICH
BELLETIER'S IS LOCATED
as a uniformed policeman and plainclothesmen investigate door
after door to find the source of the alarms ringing all over the
Square.

EXT   MEDIUM SHOT   PARKING LOT NEAR BELLETIER'S
NIGHT   GUS'S CAR
as Dix lowers Louis into the seat and shuts the door.

LOUIS

Gus, take me home.

GUS

I heard the shot. How bad is it?

LOUIS

In the thigh. I could feel it going up. I think I got the slug in
my belly.

GUS

I'll take you to a fellow I know. Used to be a doctor.

LOUIS

No, no! Take me home, Gus! I got to go home!

Beyond them, Dix and Doc walk a short distance away and get into
Louis's car. Dix takes the wheel.

MEDIUM SHOT   PARKING LOT   DOC AND DIX IN THE F.G.

toward Gus's car as he pulls past and out of the parking lot. Louis,
his face dead-white, grasps the side of the car with both hands as
they turn. There is a sound of talking and laughter, and as Gus's car
pulls out of the way, a group of half a dozen people enter the
parking lot, walking slowly in front of Dix and Doc. In the B.G., next
to the parking lot, is the movie theater, which is emptying its
audience after the last show.

MEDIUM CLOSE SHOT   PARKING LOT

people walking by in front of Dix's car. A couple stop directly in
front of the car, and the man hugs the woman and is about to kiss
her. The lights of Dix's car switch on.

MAN

Say—what's the idea?

The car starts forward, and they hastily get out of the way.

DISSOLVE TO:

INT   EMMERICH'S COTTAGE   LIVING ROOM   NIGHT

The blinds are drawn. Brannom is sitting on the sofa with a drink in
his hand. Emmerich paces the floor nervously.

EMMERICH

It's past one. They'll be here any minute.—Unless there
was trouble.

BRANNOM

Where's Angela?

EMMERICH

At her sister's.

BRANNOM

She says!

EMMERICH

I'd go easy on the liquor if I were you.

BRANNOM
Half drunk I've got better wits than most people and more
nerve.

He opens his jacket, takes a Navy .45 out of his shoulder holster,
checks the magazine, then stows the automatic between the leather
cushions on the couch.

BRANNOM
You look worried, my friend. Is something bothering
you?
(Emmerich shakes his head)
Live and learn. All these years, I've been suffering from an
inferiority complex. I should have been in the money
years ago. You big boys—what have you got? Front—
nothing but front—and when that slips . . .

O.S. the sound of an engine. Emmerich goes to the window; looks
out, sees the lights of a car on the driveway.

BRANNOM
(mockingly)
I do believe our guests are arriving.

Emmerich goes quickly to the door; opens it, and stands aside for
the little doctor followed by Dix to enter. The lawyer nods at the
small leather handbag Doc is carrying.

EMMERICH
Everything went well?

Doc holds the little bag up and nods, smiling. Brannom steps into
the hallway. Doc looks him up and down, the smile fading from his
face.

EMMERICH
This is Mr. Brannom. He's been most helpful to me in
regard to this deal.

Dix and Brannom regard each other silently—taking each other's
measure.

EMMERICH
Will you follow me, gentlemen?
(pleasantly)
It's more comfortable in here.
(he points at the little bag)
Full of Kohinoors and Grand Moguls, I hope.

DOC

Could be . . .

INT   MEDIUM SHOT   LIVING ROOM
Brannom saunters to the couch where his gun is hidden.

EMMERICH
Sit down. Sit down, gentlemen. I'll get you a drink.

DOC
No, thanks.
He sets the little bag down on the table.

EMMERICH
(clears his throat nervously)
Do you mind if we take a look?

DOC
(unstrapping the bag)
You're entitled to a look, naturally.
Slowly and carefully he turns the bag upside down. Diamonds,
rubies, and star sapphires slide into view. A heavy silence follows.
The men all stare motionless at the huge, glittering treasure scattered on the table before them. Finally the little doctor breaks the
spell. Chuckling, nervously, he holds the mouth of the bag below
the edge of the table, and begins to scoop the gems back into it.

DOC
Convinced?

EMMERICH
(jovially)
Of course. Of course. But there's never been any doubt in
my mind knowing your reputation, Riedenschneider. A
mere matter of curiosity—nothing more. I'm sure the ap-
praisal will exceed your . . .

DOC
(interrupting)
Good. Good. In that case—I'd just like to see the color of
your money.

EMMERICH
(clearing his throat pretentiously)
Gentlemen, I must say that at this moment I find myself a
bit embarrassed.

DOC
(very quietly)
You mean you haven't got the money, Mr. Emmerich?

EMMERICH
I have it—that is—I have the assurance of it.

DOC
(his eyes showing a sudden glitter)
You haven't got it!

EMMERICH
I haven't got the currency here in my hands, but it's promised by an unimpeachable source. I'm sorry. I guess we were all too anxious and moved too fast.

DOC
We moved on your word.
(Doc begins to strap up the bag)

EMMERICH
The sum is a very large one considering present-day conditions, and the fact that it is wanted in cash. So a few more days are needed to raise it.

DOC

A few more days may not seem like a very long time to you, Mr. Emmerich, but to me—carrying this around—it would seem like years.

EMMERICH
(sagely)
I quite understand. But I have a solution for that. That is, of course, if you boys trust me. If you don't—then there's nothing I can say except I am sorry.

There is a brief pause while he takes out his handerkerchief and slowly mops his brow; eyeing Dix and the little doctor.

DOC

Mr. Emmerich, what are you trying to tell us?

EMMERICH

The jewels—it's very dangerous for you to carry them around. You just said so.

DOC

You mean we leave them with you.

EMMERICH

When the police start looking for them tomorrow, will they call me up—or send detectives around to my house?
(he laughs and gestures expansively)
But you, Doctor, you're just out of prison and they're going to start looking for big-timers like yourself. Some detective may even be smart enough to connect this million-dollar robbery and your release.

Riedenschneider stands staring up at Emmerich with bleak, frosty eyes. The lawyer's nerve begins to desert him.

EMMERICH

Well, there you are.
(he makes a quick gesture intended to end all con-
troversy)
But of course—as I said—it's up to you. Take the jewels. Have Cobby keep in touch with me. Maybe by the end of the week . . .

Doc reaches for the bag.

BRANNOM
(harshly)
You did a great job, Emmerich, but it's not working—
so . . .

They all turn to him at once. He is sitting on the edge of the sofa staring hard at Dix and Doc. In his right hand is the Navy .45. His face is pale, but his jaw is set. He looks grimly determined.

EMMERICH
(in a shocked voice)
Bob!

BRANNOM
(his eyes on Dix and Doc)
Back away and keep out of this, Emmerich.

Emmerich obeys, backing away behind an easy chair.

BRANNOM
(to Dix)
Now you—farmer! Get your hands up.
(glancing at the Doc)
And you—Fritz—throw the bag on the floor. Over here by my feet. And be careful how you throw it. I got a pistol expert medal.

MEDIUM SHOT   BRANNOM'S HAND HOLDING THE PISTOL
in the immediate F.G., toward Doc and Dix. Doc glances sideways at Dix who, his face expressionless, is slowly raising his hands.

DOC
What do you say, Dix?

BRANNOM
He's got no say. If he makes a crooked move, he'll never pitch another forkful of manure.

DIX
Toss him the bag, Doc. He's got us.

BRANNOM
You're not as dumb as you look.

There's a brief pause, then Doc Riedenschneider tosses the bag toward Brannom with both hands. Simultaneously, Dix pulls his own revolver from the waistband of his trousers and jumps sideways. Both guns, Dix's and Brannom's in the immediate F.G., roar at the same time.

MEDIUM SHOT   EMMERICH
He turns and crouches behind the protection of the easy chair, his
face dead-white.

MEDIUM CLOSE SHOT   BRANNOM
He is staring stupidly into space. His gun drops from his fingers
and he himself slides off the settee and down to his knees, and then
slowly onto his face into the rug.

MEDIUM CLOSE SHOT   DOC
stooping forward to recover the briefcase, turns from Brannom to
look back toward Dix.

MEDIUM CLOSE SHOT   DIX
He has staggered back against the wall and is pressing his left hand
to his left side. There is a long ragged tear in his coat.

FULL SHOT   PAST EMMERICH
kneeling behind the chair, toward the other three men, one
wounded, one dying. Dix, the gun still in his hand crosses the room
toward him, slowly. He pushes aside the shelter of the easy chair
with one foot. Emmerich has crouched down, almost flat on his
face.

                              DIX
            Are you a man? Or what? Trying to gyp and double-cross,
            but with no guts for it. What's inside of you? What's
            keeping you alive?
Emmerich rises slowly from his knees. A strange expression passes
over his death-like face—an expression compounded of resigna-
tion, dignity, and sudden resolution. His jaw shows a certain
firmness, and the lines at his mouth are hard. He regards Dix coldly
and without fear.

                         EMMERICH
            Go ahead—kill me. What's stopping you?
Dix moves a step closer to the lawyer—leveling his weapon. Then
Doc runs up from behind and talking rapidly pushes the barrel
down.

                             DOC
            Dix, listen to me—don't kill him. It's too easy an out for
            him.
Dix leans against the wall, one hand pressing against his side.

DOC
Whatever possessed you, Mr. Emmerich, to pull such a stunt?

EMMERICH
I was broke—facing bankruptcy.

DIX
Doc, he's a witness. He saw me knock off that guy there. You think he wouldn't holler if they turned the heat on him.

DOC
He's in no positon to talk.
(turning to Emmerich)
What did you and your man there on the floor intend to do with the jewels?

EMMERICH
Leave town—sell them off—a little at a time.

DOC
No good. The police would have been on you after the first sale. You can't go peddling stuff like this around when the heat's on.

DIX
Let's blow, Doc. Let's not fool around here any longer.

DOC
Be patient, Dix. Mr. Emmerich got us into this hole and he's going to get us out.
(to Emmerich)
I didn't save your life because I'm a lover of humanity. We're in trouble with this satchel full of jewels. As things stand, it's just so much junk.

EMMERICH
There's nothing I can do.

DOC
Yes there is, Mr. Emmerich. You can go to the insurance company.

EMMERICH
Insurance company . . . ?
(he nods)

DOC

They'll listen to reason. This is a very bad jolt for them, and it's possible they'd be willing to buy the jewels back—no questions asked—for as high as twenty-five percent of what they're worth.

DIX

Doc, let's blow.

EMMERICH

I'll start on it tomorrow.

DOC

Get busy, Emmerich, and remember you might have been lying here dead with your friend.

EMMERICH

Should I get in touch with you through Cobby?

DOC

No. I will get in touch with you. Come on, Dix.

They start out.

DOC

(at the hall door; briefly)

I advise you to clean up after your friend.

They go out, Dix closing the door. Emmerich is left alone with the body. Outside there are the sounds of a car door opening and closing, the engine starting, the car pulling away. Emmerich kneels down, reaches under the body, and drawing out Brannom's gun, puts it into his own pocket. Then, taking out his handerchief, he begins frantically to wipe every object, every surface, that could possibly have a fingerprint.

DISSOLVE TO:

INT   MEDIUM SHOT   THE CIAVELLI KITCHEN   NIGHT
CAMERA PANNING WITH MARIA CIAVELLI as she fills a glass of water and takes it toward the bedroom. In the F.G. is Gus, sitting on a kitchen chair, his unnaturally long arms bent like a frog's, and his thick hands rubbing his knees.

GUS

Don't give him water.

Maria disregards him, going past the baby's crib, which has been pulled into the kitchen, and into the doorway to the bedroom. Louis Ciavelli is visible in the semi-darkness, groaning, lying on one side. Gus gets up, tries to wrest the glass away from Maria.

> MARIA
>
> He asked for it. Let go!

> GUS
>
> I said don't give him water. You want to kill him? Maybe he's hurt in the stomach.

The water spills on the floor. Maria pulls away from him.

> MARIA
>
> Where's the doctor? Why doesn't he come? You told me ten minutes—it's half an hour. Louis'll die. Why can't I take my Louis to the hospital?

> GUS
>
> You take him to the hospital—they wheel him into the operating room—you never see him again.

Maria begins to wring her hands and sway.

> GUS
>
> Take it easy, Louis'll be all right. The doctor will fix him up as good as new. You and Louis will have six more kids—and everyone fat as a pig with big black eyes and lots of hair. Just like Louis, eh, Maria?

He bends over the crib, and pokes a thick, hairy finger at the baby.

> MARIA
> (shouting)
> Stay away from the baby!

Gus slowly retreats, scowling, sits down with back to Maria.

> MARIA
>
> Tell me the truth, Gus—how did it happen?

> GUS
> (sullenly)
> I told you—a fight.

> MARIA
>
> Louis don't fight. You know that.

Gus shrugs.

MARIA

Why is it always you? Whenever he gets into trouble
you're around—why?
          (the Italian peasant)
You crooked back—You dirty cripple—You have the evil
eye!
Gus gets up—in sudden violence.

GUS

Maria, don't say that! I don't like anybody to say that!

MARIA

I'm sorry, Gus, but I got to blame somebody.

GUS

What I carry on my back—I was born with it—I didn't
grow it myself.

MARIA

Please, Gus. I'm sorry. Forgive me, Gus. I didn't mean it.
There is a silence between them. Maria lifts the baby out of the crib
to comfort herself rather than the baby. In the next room, Louis
shifts in the bed and grunts with pain. There is the sound of distant
sirens.

MARIA

Listen to that!

GUS

Yeah. Must be a fire—but not around here—not in this
neighborhood.

MARIA

Oh, Gus—I pray God to send that doctor here quick.

GUS
          (no longer angry)
He ought to be here any minute, Maria.

MARIA

Sounds like a soul in hell . . .

                                        DISSOLVE TO:

EXT   MEDIUM SHOT   THE BRIDGE OVER THE RIVER   NIGHT
as Emmerich's car comes to a stop in the center of the span. He gets

out, opens the door on Brannom's side. Then he looks up. The lights of a trolley are approaching, rattling and empty except for a few sleepy passengers. Emmerich walks around the car and crouches behind it, shielding his face as the trolley passes. Then, when it is over the bridge, he pulls Brannom's body out of the car, lifts it to the height of the guard rail, and lets it roll out of the blanket.

EXT   MEDIUM SHOT   FROM FAR ABOVE   THE SURFACE OF THE RIVER   NIGHT
as Brannom's body falls loosely, absurdly into the water, and is carried downstream, under the shadow of the bridge.

DISSOLVE TO:

INT   FULL SHOT   COBBY'S OFFICE   NIGHT
Cobby is walking back and forth—frantic with worry. His face is pale and drawn. From time to time, he groans faintly. Dix, his shirt off, is sitting sideways on a straight chair. He is swabbing his wound with a big hunk of cotton dipped in iodine. The little doctor is at a card table. He still wears his hat and overcoat. The bag containing the jewels is on the table. He keeps sliding it around and around idly.

DOC
Dix, you'd better get in touch with Gus, and let him take you to that doctor. Don't be foolish.

DIX
I don't like doctors. I'm getting along all right. The bullet just ripped through my side and went on about its business. Good thing I jumped.

COBBY
How can things go so wrong . . . . How is it possible?—One man killed, two other guys plugged. I'm out thirty grand and we got a load of rocks we can't peddle.

DIX
(interrupting)
Quit crying and get me some bourbon, will you?
Cobby pours drinks for both Dix and himself.

COBBY
(whining)
I must be awful stupid. Here I am with a good business—money rolling in, and I get myself mixed up in a thing like this. I ought to have my head examined!

The telephone rings. Cobby answers it.

COBBY

Hello. Yeah. This is Cobby.
　　　(startled)
. . . What? . . .
　　　(turning to Doc and Dix)
. . . It's Gus.—Dragnet's out—they're combing the district. He wants to talk to you, Dix.

Dix crosses the room; jerks the receiver away from Cobby.

DIX

Gus . . . Dix.

GUS'S VOICE
　　　(over phone)
Listen careful, pal. The coppers are knocking over all the joints along the boulevard—mobs of them!—meatwagons and all!

CUT TO:

INT　CLOSE SHOT　GUS'S RESTAURANT

GUS
　　　(at phone)
Now look—I already called a guy—Eddie Donato. He's got a grocery down by the river—116 Front Street—get that?—okay.

DIX'S VOICE

Thanks, Gus. How's Louis?

GUS

Louis's not so good.—Slug in his belly all right. The Doc's doing all he can.

Through the window, Gus sees a police wagon and a police car pull up. Two uniformed policemen and a plainclothesman get out of the car and come toward the door.

GUS

Here they are now.—The Happiness Boys. Guess I'm in for a working over. Look, go to Eddie's by way of the Old Market. At night it's deserted. When you get beyond the market, you'll be safe. The cops never bother Eddie's neighborhood. So long, Dix. Blow now!

The police are rapping at the front door when Gus hangs up. He grimly looks at it. It almost gives way under a hammering blow.

GUS

Okay, okay!

He takes a deep breath and goes to open the door as we

DISSOLVE TO:

INT   FULL SHOT   SMALL ROOM AT POLICE HEADQUARTERS
EARLY MORNING

Four or five girls, among them Doll, are grouped in this barren reception room waiting for their turn to be questioned in an adjacent room, the door to which is closed.

BIG GIRL

It's that commissioner. I saw his picture in the paper. He looks like an old billy goat, only he ain't got any beard. All he does is make trouble.

FAT WOMAN

You said a mouthful, honey. Why can't he leave us alone.

The door opens and a police lieutenant in uniform steps in.

LIEUTENANT
(pointing)

All right, you and you, in here!

Doll and another girl, Vivian, go through into the other room. The lieutenant follows them in, closes the door behind him.

GROUP SHOT   THREE OR FOUR REMAINING GIRLS

A THIN GIRL

What's the beef, anyway? We got to eat, don't we?

BIG GIRL

Just because he's all for morality and stuff like that—that don't change the world, does it?

We hear a woman's voice, raised in anger, shouting unintelligibly.

CUT TO:

INT   FULL SHOT   ADJACENT ROOM   EARLY MORNING

The room is blocked and crowded with a long table, straight chairs, several steel files; a single light is on, though through a narrow window, a grey misty dawn is beginning to reveal the streets beyond. A lieutenant in uniform is questioning Vivian. In the F.G., huddled into his overcoat, Commissioner Hardy listens.

LIEUTENANT
(holding out a photograph)
All right, Vivian. Take it easy. All we want to know is have
you ever seen this man?

VIVIAN
I ain't seen anybody. I been sick in bed. I was dragged out
of a sick bed and thrown in the wagon.

LIEUTENANT
Okay, Vivian. Run along.
She is led out. The lieutenant looks up at Hardy.

HARDY
Keep it up. We'll get somewhere. His signature's all over
this job.
Doll is led in.

LIEUTENANT
Doll Conovan?

DOLL
That's right.

LIEUTENANT
Ever see this man at any time in the last ten days?

DOLL
I guess not.

LIEUTENANT
You *guess* not! What do you mean? Did you or didn't you?

DOLL
I mean I guess I didn't.

LIEUTENANT
Look again! Take a good look!
INSERT: POLICE PHOTO OF RIEDENSCHNEIDER

DOLL
Nossir.

LIEUTENANT
Nossir—what?

DOLL
I just don't guess I ever met him.
The lieutenant jerks his head permitting Doll to leave. CAMERA DOLLIES WITH HER down a bleak, grey hall to the door of the station house. Then HOLDS on her forlorn figure as she walks out up the street in the cold light of dawn.

DISSOLVE TO:

INT   MEDIUM SHOT   CONFERENCE ROOM ON HIGH FLOOR, INSURANCE BUILDING   BRIGHT DAY
The room has a long conference table and twelve leather chairs, only three of which are occupied at the moment: one by Emmerich who wears the marks, under his immaculate shave, of a night's sleeplessness; one, by a bold, peppery, rather pompous man in a black suit, an insurance executive named James X. Connery; the third by Maxwell, his superior.

CONNERY
You have no doubt about the—legitimacy—of the offer?

EMMERICH
None at all.—And I speak with some knowledge of underworld methods. . . . Well, gentlemen, what shall I report when they call back?

MAXWELL
I'm against it—on principle!

EMMERICH
I understand your feelings, Mr. Maxwell. They do you credit. Far better your insurance company take a million dollar loss than deal with thieves—if it can afford to.

MAXWELL
(clears his throat)
This isn't something we can decide by ourselves, we'll have to consult with others in the firm.

EMMERICH
You understand of course that I would want nothing—absolutely nothing in the way of a fee. I prefer to regard what I'd be doing as a public service.

CONNERY
(shaking hands)
Very generous of you, Mr. Emmerich.
Emmerich goes out.

MAXWELL
How crooked can you get?
(he thinks for a moment, folds his long, white
beautifully manicured hands, then flicks a switch
and speaks into the dictograph)
Get me Police Commissioner Hardy.

CONNERY
Hold on—use your head! Suppose we do nail Emmerich.
That wouldn't say the jewelry would be recovered.

MAXWELL
You're quite right. It doesn't.

CONNERY
I know it's bad practice, but a million dollars . . .

MAXWELL
. . . is a lot of money.

CONNERY
Remember that big jewelry theft in the East—the Shafter
job? Sure, the police caught the criminals, but it took four
years and we only recovered about ten percent of what
was stolen. Emmerich's gang will settle for twenty-five
percent. Look at it as a matter of simple arithmetic.
A buzzer SOUNDS.

MAXWELL
Yes?

SECRETARY
(over speaker)
Commissioner Hardy—on two, Mr. Maxwell.
Maxwell picks up the receiver.

MAXWELL
Commissioner?—Maxwell of Mid-City Insurance—Is
there any progress, so far? I see—I see—thank you, sir.—I
appreciate your frankness—Goodbye, Commissioner.
He hangs up. They haven't got a thing.

CONNERY
(relieved)
I thought maybe you were going to tell him about Emmerich.

MAXWELL
Certainly not. I just wanted to know how things stood before giving that crook Emmerich the go-ahead sign.

DISSOLVE TO:

EXT   LONG SHOT   TENEMENT DISTRICT NEAR RIVER   DAY
An Italian grocery store on corner. Children are playing a skipping game in the street. CAMERA MOVES UP to window on the second floor—enters a room.

INT   FULL SHOT   EDDIE DONATO'S UPSTAIRS ROOM   DAY
Doc is asleep on one of the cots, his coat and shoes off and one hand hanging limp against the floor. Dix is standing moodily looking out the window, which looks into the narrow street that descends to the river. There's a knock at door. Dix turns slowly around, then Doc wakes and sits up. Neither moves any further.

VOICE OUTSIDE DOOR
It's me—Eddie Donato.
Dix goes and lets him in. He carries two platters heaped with gleaming spaghetti.

DONATO
You like spaghetti? I make it very good. Plenty of oregano—smell it?

DIX
Sure. Put it down. Thanks.
Donato puts both plates down on the dresser—the nearest thing to a table in the room.

DOC
Anybody call us?

DONATO
No calls. Everything's nice and quiet.

DOC
I don't know why we don't hear from Cobby.

DIX

Come on, Doc. Sit down and eat.

Doc sighs, draws up a chair. Dix eats standing.

DOC

Real spaghetti—great. I ate it by the yard in Naples.

DIX

(to Donato)

What size shirt you wear?

DONATO

Me?—I wear a fifteen. But I buy a sixteen and a half
because I like lots of room. Same with underwear and
pajamas. I always wear pajamas. In the old country,
people sleep in underwear—a very dirty habit.

DIX

How about me buying a couple of shirts from you?

DONATO

Sure. Sure. What color you like? I got pink, yellow,
salmon—very pretty—

                         DIX
How about brown or white?

                       DONATO
That's no color—brown, white.

                         DIX
Okay. Anything you got.

                       DONATO
I got light blue, purple—
The phone rings somewhere outside the room. Donato goes to the
door, opens it, and goes down a short staircase to the street floor,
where a pay telephone is hung on the thickly painted wall. Doc
stops eating, but Dix goes methodically on.

                       DONATO
                 (off into phone)
Yeah? What? Talk louder! I don't get the name!
Dix puts his fork down, too. Doc stands up, goes to the open door at
the head of the staircase, Dix follows him.

INT   MEDIUM SHOT   SHOOTING DOWN STAIRCASE TOWARD
TELEPHONE   DAY
In the F.G. wait Doc and Dix.

                       DONATO
Sure—sure—I'll get him for you.
He motions for Doc to come down. Doc descends, lifts the receiver.

                         DOC
Hello—yes?—Fine, fine.—Good.—That will be satisfac-
tory.
He hangs up, goes silently up the steps, enters and closes the door.

MEDIUM TWO-SHOT   THE UPSTAIRS ROOM

                         DIX
Cobby?

                         DOC
Yes. Emmerich came through. The insurance people say
okay. Of course, we'll have to wait till the banks open—
Monday morning. But it's two hundred fifty thousand.
Which is not bad!
Dix nods, walks back and begins to eat his spaghetti again.

> DIX
>
> Two more days!—Wish I had a T-bone steak.

DISSOLVE TO:

INT MRS. EMMERICH'S BEDROOM NIGHT
She and Emmerich are playing cassino. He is sitting on the side of her bed. She has on a new bed-jacket of padded silk, and her brushed hair falls becomingly around her shoulders. In her happiness and excitement over the card game, she is, despite her years, an attractive woman.

> MRS. EMMERICH
> (laughing triumphantly)
>
> As a lawyer you may be very brilliant, Lon—but as a cassino player you have a lot to learn.

> EMMERICH
> (smiles)
>
> Mind if I smoke?

> MRS. EMMERICH
>
> Of course not, Lon.

He plays a card and takes out a cigar.

> MRS. EMMERICH
>
> Oh, Lon! How could you make such a play as that? You won't make a single point this hand.

He is striking a match when there is a discreet knock at the door. The butler enters.

> EMMERICH
>
> Yes?

> BUTLER
>
> Two gentlemen to see you, sir—from the police department.

Emmerich freezes in the act of lighting the cigar. The hand holding the match begins to tremble.

> MRS. EMMERICH
>
> What on earth can they want, Lon?

> EMMERICH
>
> Something to do with a case probably.

MRS. EMMERICH
Oh bother!—we're having so much fun. Hurry back!
Emmerich goes out of the room.

CUT TO:

LONG SHOT   SHOOTING DOWN THE STAIRS TO
two plainclothesmen standing in the roomy hall.

EMMERICH enters from BEHIND CAMERA—starts down the stairs.

CUT TO:

LONG SHOT   EMMERICH
descending the stairs. The plainclothesmen are in the F.G.—their hats are off. Nobody speaks until Emmerich reaches the bottom of the stairs.

HANNIGAN
Sorry to disturb you, Mr. Emmerich. I'm Hannigan. This is Officer Janocek.

EMMERICH
What can I do for you?

HANNIGAN
Do you know a man named Robert Brannom?

EMMERICH
Yes, I do. Why? Is something the matter?

HANNIGAN
There sure is, Mr. Emmerich. His body was pulled out of the river this morning.

EMMERICH
Great heavens!

HANNIGAN
But it was no drowning. He had a hole through his pump—he'd been shot.

EMMERICH
Come in here, gentlemen.
He leads the way into the cardroom.

FULL SHOT   THE CARDROOM IN EMMERICH'S HOUSE
as he enters with the detectives.

EMMERICH

Sit down. This is quiet a shock. Bob Brannom murdered—great heavens!

HANNIGAN
(taking out a folded slip of paper)
We found a list of names in his pocket—written on your
business stationery. Who are these people, do you know?

EMMERICH

That's a list of my debtors. Brannom was working for
me—trying to collect old debts without much success.

HANNIGAN
Was he giving the treatment to anybody on this list?

EMMERICH
Certainly not!

HANNIGAN
Then you don't think there was any connection between
this work you say he was doing for you—and his death?

EMMERICH
None whatever.

JANOCEK
When did you see him last?

EMMERICH
Wednesday evening—in this room.—We checked that list
over together.

JANOCEK
The coroner says he was plugged about one or two o'clock
this morning—not much after the Belletier job was pulled.
We figure there might be a connection.
(Emmerich frowns thoughtfully)
One of the heist guys was shot. We know that. There was
blood on the floor. Maybe it was Brannom's. He could
have died in the getaway car, and the others dropped him
in the river.

EMMERICH
Not a chance—Brannom was something of a roughneck,
but he wasn't a criminal—and if I'm any judge, Belletier's
was the work of big-time professionals.

(shakes his head)
No, gentlemen—Bob's taking part in that or any other burglary is inconceivable.

ANDREWS
I see.
They get up.

ANDREWS
One more thing, Mr. Emmerich. Just for the records, of course. Could you give us an account of your whereabouts, Friday night?

EMMERICH
I could, but it would be rather embarrassing. Is it necessary?

ANDREWS
I'm afraid so, Mr. Emmerich.

EMMERICH
As a man in his fifties, I hate to make this admission. A young lady named Angela Finlay is living at my cottage on the river. I went to see her last night—about eleven-thirty, I think it was—then I stayed later than I intended. She will confirm this, I think. But, boys, use your discretion. If it serves no useful purpose—

ANDREWS
I understand, Mr. Emmerich. And thank you very much for your help.

EMMERICH
If I can be of any further assistance, please call me.
(he leads them to the door)
Good night, gentlemen.

DETECTIVES
'Night, Mr. Emmerich.
They go out. Emmerich turns, and picking up the phone, he dials a number.

EMMERICH
Angela?—This is Lon.—Look, Baby, you may get a visit from the police—no, nothing to be alarmed about—certainly not. They may ask you some questions about last

Friday night—and I want you to tell them I was with
you—most of the night—from eleven-twenty to three in
the morning.—Is that clear, Baby? No, it's just politics,
good old dirty politics.—I'll call you later. Goodbye.
Hanging up the receiver, Emmerich turns and starts back up the
stairs.

INT   MRS. EMMERICH'S BEDROOM
Hearing Emmerich's step on the stair, she makes an involuntary
gesture toward arranging her hair. Emmerich enters.

> MRS. EMMERICH
Can we go on playing?

> EMMERICH
All right.
He sits down on the bed. Her face shows concern.

> MRS. EMMERICH
Why, you're as pale as a ghost. What's the matter?

> EMMERICH
I heard some bad news. Man who was working for me got
killed.

> MRS. EMMERICH
Oh, Lon, how awful! Was it an accident?

> EMMERICH
> (shakes his head)
No. It was an intentional killing.

> MRS. EMMERICH
What was his name?

> EMMERICH
Brannom. He had a private detective agency.

> MRS. EMMERICH
Do they know who did it?
> (Emmerich shakes his head)
Lon, when I think about all those awful people you come
into contact with—downright criminals—I get scared.

> EMMERICH
There's nothing so different about them.
Something in his tone strikes her as queer. Watching him, she
frowns slightly.

EMMERICH
—After all, crime is only a left-handed form of human
endeavor.

She is studying his face as we:

DISSOLVE TO:

INSERT: DOC'S PHOTOGRAPH THREE COLUMNS WIDE SET
SQUARELY IN THE MIDDLE OF THE FRONT PAGE OF THE EVENING
CHRONICLE

CAMERA PULLS BACK TO:

CLOSE SHOT   EDDIE DONATO IN HIS STORE   NIGHT
as his eyes involuntarily look toward the ceiling. In the B.G., a
fourteen-year-old boy is sweeping up. Donato lowers the paper,
stands undecided for a long moment then moves hesitantly toward
the stairs.

INT   MEDIUM SHOT   UPSTAIRS ROOM   DIX AND DOC
Doc is sitting by the window, smoking a cigar, and looking at the
lights on the river. Dix is stretched out on the cot.

DOC
Ever been in Mexico City, Dix?

DIX
(without opening his eyes)
Nope.

DOC
It's eight thousand feet up. The air is very pure—many
first-class clubs and restaurants—a horse track—and
girls—plenty young girls. How would you like to go
there—all expenses paid?

DIX
(laconically)
Sorry, Doc—not interested. I'm heading South. ⦁

DOC
Listen, Dix: You can always go home, and when you
do—it's nothing. Believe me, I've done it—nothing.

DIX
My mind's made up, Doc.

There is the sound of feet on the bare floor outside in the hall. Dix
jumps up quickly; jerks his gun and stands waiting. Then there is
the sound of scratching on the door. Eddie's voice comes softly O.S.

EDDIE
(O.S.)
It's me.

Dix puts away his gun and opens the door.

Donato steps in quickly as if pursued. He glances over his shoulder into the dark hallway as Dix closes the door behind him. Then he holds out the paper pathetically.

EDDIE
Look, my friends—

Dix takes the paper from Eddie's trembling hands. Doc comes over to Dix, seeing the front page, he whistles softly.

EDDIE
(tears in his voice)
I'm a respectable man. For Gus I do a favor all right, but please . . . . With this picture in the paper . . . .

DIX
You mean you want us to blow? Is that right, Eddie?

Eddie shrinks back, but continues to plead.

EDDIE
Please—How can I get mixed up in a thing like this? I can't live, my friends—I can't live . . . !

DIX
(shutting him off)
Okay, Eddie.
(to Doc)
The sooner we blow the better. Our friend Eddie's getting to the place where he'd talk with a little encouragement.

EDDIE
Oh no. I no talk. Gus cut my belly open. I go now, my friends. I'm sorry to bring you this bad news, but . . .

DIX
(breaks in coldly)
You sit down. You're not going any place till I say so.

Eddie stares at Dix in horror. Then he makes a quick dart for the door, but Dix grabs him by the back of his shirt and heaves him across the room and on to the bed.

A Screenplay 99

                    DIX

Stay put, Eddie. Nobody's going to hurt you if you sit still
and keep your mouth shut.

There is a long silence broken only by Eddie's heavy breathing.
Doc, who has not stopped studying the newspaper, shakes his
head.

                    DIX

The way I figure—the insurance guys sicked the cops on to
that big phony—and he spilled. You shouldn't have
stopped me, Doc, when I was going to blast him.

                    DOC
         (drops the paper; starts putting on his overcoat)
No, Dix, he hasn't spilled. Or they wouldn't be looking for
just me.

                    DIX

Then how come?

                    DOC

Because there's only four or five men who could manage a
job like this. Somebody in the department with a few
brains has decided I'm the guy. I've been half expecting it.
It doesn't worry me much. We'll get our money tomorrow,
you bet.

                    DIX

Hope so. . . . Come on, Doc. Let's go.

                    DOC

Where can we go, Dix?

                    DIX
         (recalling)
I know a place.

He feels in his pockets, brings out the match cover Doll wrote her
new address on; then, he turns to the man on the bed.

                    DIX

Eddie, if you're a smart boy you'll forget you ever seen us.

                    EDDIE

I say nothing to nobody. Don't worry about that, Mister.

Dix and the little doctor leave without speaking again, closing the door softly behind them. Eddie hurries on tip-toe, and stands with his ear pressed to the door. Presently he heaves a long sigh of relief.

DISSOLVE TO:

EXT   MEDIUM LONG SHOT   DESERTED BOULEVARD   NIGHT
Doc and Dix jaywalk over the wide thoroughfare. Doc carries the briefcase. On the opposite side of the street is a huge, ponderous, arcade-like structure, an old market, stretching for nearly three blocks, but condemned, and now partially open to the weather. Dix and Doc enter the building through a broken doorway.

INT   MEDIUM LONG SHOT   THE OLD MARKET   NIGHT
The only illumination is far overhead—a faint glow from the street—lights through the broken windows. Dix and Doc are no more than shadowy silhouettes, their feet shuffling through a litter of old newspapers on the floor. On the river nearby, a tug moans on its way upstream, the sound echoing hollowly through the big empty building. As the two figures approach the CAMERA, they are suddenly illuminated in the circle of light from the beam of a torch. They both freeze. The hand holding the searchlight emerges into the F.G., the cuff identifies it as part of a policeman's uniform.

                    POLICEMAN
Where do you guys think you're going?

                    DIX
We're on our way home.

                    POLICEMAN
Where do you live?

                    DIX
South on Camden.

                    POLICEMAN
Well—you guys got no business in here—city property. There are signs all over the place.

                    DIX
Everybody uses it.

                    POLICEMAN
You're telling me. Bunch of hoodlums been bringing young girls in here.

DOC
(interested at once)
Is that a fact?

MEDIUM CLOSE THREE-SHOT, PAST DOC AND DIX
toward the policeman with the flashlight. Dix and Doc begin to go
past him toward the street about ten feet beyond. The policeman
plays his beam over the backs of Dix and then Doc, then switches it
off.

POLICEMAN
Yeah. It's already cost one of us boys his job on account of
the beefs. If I was you guys I'd stay out of here—
understand?

DIX
Okay, officer.
The beam from the torch goes on again, playing over the doctor.

POLICEMAN
Wait a minute! It seems to me . . . ! Come outside with
me.
In the F.G., he puts the flashlight in his left hand, reaches around
and pulls out his gun. There is a creak of holster leather. Dix
turning, leaps at the policeman straight down the beam from the
torch. There is a violent shock of bodies, the flashlight goes out as it
strikes the floor. Missing the gun hand with his first grab, Dix
strikes two hard blows into the policeman's stomach. The gun in
the policeman's hand swings widely, trying to pull free. Doc jumps
toward the two men, but just in time to be struck by the flailing gun.
He stumbles backward into a pile of debris. In the half-darkness,
there is the sickening sound of hard blows, struck with the metal
object. There is a shuffling among the debris on the floor, the
flashlight goes on, and is held by Dix, who has the policeman's gun
in his left hand, the barrel gripped like a club. He throws it away
from him. Then he runs the beam along the floor till he finds Doc
Riedenschneider, lying full length in a pile of old newspapers.
CAMERA, PANS WITH DIX as he pulls Doc up to his knees, then to
his feet.

DIX
Come on, Doc. Got the stuff?

Doc, still groggy, mutters unintelligibly. Dix reaches down to find that the Doc still has the briefcase clutched in his right hand. Supporting the Doc with one arm, Dix switches off the flashlight and hurls it away.

CAMERA PANS WITH THEM as they move quickly toward the street.

DISSOLVE TO:

INT   FULL SHOT   COMMISSIONER HARDY'S OUTER OFFICE
NIGHT
Many people are crowded in the room. A taxidriver, a thin, pale, man with a cap in his hand, has just entered the room. He comes face to face with the commissioner's secretary, a big, young man in an immaculate uniform.

SECRETARY
Yeah?

TAXIDRIVER
I want to see the commissioner.

SECRETARY
State your business.

TAXIDRIVER
Look, I'm a citizen. Can't I see the commissioner if I want to?

SECRETARY
Is it about Riedenschneider?

TAXIDRIVER
Could be.

SECRETARY
He sure gets around, that guy. About five thousand people have seen him in the last twenty-four hours. Look, buddy, the commissioner's pretty busy these days. If you just get on that line over there and wait your turn you can tell your story.

TAXIDRIVER
I won't tell nobody but the commissioner.

SECRETARY
(sighing)
Okay, buddy. Sit down and wait. But it may be some
time.

DISSOLVE TO:

INT FULL SHOT DOLL'S APARTMENT NIGHT
Doll has fallen asleep across the tumbled bed, with the light still on.
There is a violent knocking at the door. Doll responds very slowly,
getting to her feet with difficulty, shuffling across the floor and then
fumbling interminably with the lock. She opens the door, stares
uncomprehendingly at Dix and Doc standing there.

DOLL
Dix—honey! You got to excuse me, I—
Supporting Doc, Dix pushes past her into the room. Doc falls into a
chair. Gasping, he clutches the bag between his knees. Dix shuts
and locks the door, draws the shades.

DOLL
I took three sleeping tablets, so I—I'm kind of groggy. I
haven't been able to sleep lately—worrying about you and
everything. I went back to your place, Dix. They told me
the cops were after you.

DIX
Get me some cold water and some towels and don't stand
there yapping.
She looks at the little doctor sitting in the chair with his face in his
hands, sees the blood on his head.

DOLL
Sure, sure, Dix honey.

DIX
Well, get a move on.

DOLL
You bet, honey—you bet.
She runs into the bathroom, stumbling in her haste.

DOC
You put in hours and hours of planning—figure everything down to the last detail—then what? Burglar alarms

start going off for no sensible reason. A gun fires of its
own accord and a man is shot. And a broken-down old
harness-bull, no good for anything but chasing kids—has
to trip over us. Blind accident! What can you do against
blind accident?

Dix helps the doctor off with his coat; helps him over to the bed.

> DOC
> One thing I ought've figured and didn't was Emmerich
> . . . and I know why I didn't. I'm not kidding myself. It
> was the extra dough he promised. I got greedy. Greed
> made me blind.

Doll comes in with the water and the towels. Dix starts to bathe the
doctor's head. Now for the first time, she sees his face. Her mouth
drops open and she gives a sudden start of recognition.

> DOLL
> Dix, isn't he the one with the reward on him?

> DIX
> Mind your own business.

> DISSOLVE TO:

INT   FULL SHOT   HARDY'S OFFICE   NIGHT
It's cold, the heat has been shut off in the old police building. Hardy
is sitting at his desk wearing his hat and his overcoat. His face has a
white stubble of beard. A half dozen police officers are in the room,
most of them in plain-clothes. Deputy Chief Andrews is standing in
front of the desk.

> ANDREWS
> She confirmed what Emmerich said.—That he was with
> her from eleven-thirty till three.

> HARDY
> How did she impress you?

> ANDREWS
> Very much—I mean—she's some babe. If he wasn't with
> her, he's nuts.

> HARDY
> (testily)
> That isn't what I mean. Was her manner straightforward?

ANDREWS
(nods)
I guess she was telling the truth all right.

HARDY
Married twenty years, and consorting with a woman
young enough to be his granddaughter. It's disgusting.
(he gets up, begins to pace the room, his hands
buried in the big pockets of his overcoat)
—But nothing could surprise me about Emmerich. An
educated man who uses his brains to circumvent the
law.—Worst type of human being. No excuse for him.
The harness-bull who acts as Hardy's secretary, sticks his head in,
clears his throat.

HARDY
Well?

SECRETARY
Excuse me, Commissioner. There's a taxidriver been waiting out here says he's got some important information.

HARDY
Concerning what?

SECRETARY
I tried to find out. But he wouldn't talk to anybody but
you. He's been waiting two hours.

HARDY
Bring him in.
The secretary makes a motion with his head. The taxidriver, his cap
still in his hands, and the match still in his mouth, enters the room.

HARDY
What's your name?

TAXIDRIVER
Charles Wright—Hackie number: 6456—Green Stripe
Company.

HARDY
What's this information you've got?

TAXIDRIVER
That little doctor everybody's looking for—I think I had
him for a fare.

HARDY

You drove him someplace?

TAXIDRIVER

Well, now, I'm pretty sure it was him I picked up at the Station—a week ago Friday.

HARDY

(snaps)

Where did you take him?

TAXIDRIVER

To a number on Camden West. I remember because I asked him if he wanted me to wait. The number was dark, see.—Well, he was a harmless-looking little guy and I felt kind of guilty leaving him at that dark number. I know a fellow got rolled on Camden West.—And he didn't have nothing so they stole his pants and shoes.

HARDY

Where did you take him—what number?

TAXIDRIVER

(consulting a notebook)

4717—it was kind of a store room—dark.

DETECTIVE

What's that number again?

TAXIDRIVER

4717.

DETECTIVE

Used to be a bookie joint, Commissioner.

HARDY

Get hold of Lieutenant Ditrich!

He opens his desk drawer, takes out a half dozen pictures, spreads them on the desk before the taxi driver. The latter's mouth drops open. He stares, hesitates, then speaks with conviction.

TAXIDRIVER

That's him, Commissioner. Yeah. I was thinking maybe I was making a fool of myself coming down here—but that's him all right.

HARDY

You may be in for a reward—I hope so.

SECRETARY'S VOICE

(over dictograph)

Lieutenant Ditrich—on one.

Hardy picks up the phone.

HARDY

Where are you, Ditrich? . . . All right . . . . Get a search warrant and go to 4717 Camden West . . . . Riedenschneider was seen there . . . . Stake your men out before you go in. Now, get a move on!

As he puts down the telephone, Officer Janocek comes into the room.

JANOCEK

Some news just came in. One of our patrolmen was on special duty at the Old Market. He ran into two men, and was slugged. They got away, but he identified the smaller one as Riedenschneider . . . .

HARDY

Good! Great! We'll block off the whole area—and no sirens! A sneak!

(he makes his way to a corner of the room, begins to pull on his rubbers, then looks up at Janocek)

What about the patrolman—badly hurt?

JANOCEK

Some nasty head wounds, they say. And he's kind of punchy, but the doctor doesn't think he's got a fracture.

Hardy nods, walks over to take hold of Andrews's arm, and they begin to leave the room.

HARDY

Well, son, looks like maybe we're getting somewhere at last!

His eyes shine with excitement behind his spectacles.

DISSOLVE TO:

INT FULL SHOT COBBY'S OFFICE NIGHT

Ditrich stands with his back to him, as Cobby pours a drink.

COBBY

Look, Lieutenant. What would I know about Belletier's? I wouldn't mix in no robbery, you know that.

DITRICH

Wouldn't you?

COBBY

No. Of course not. You saw Riedenschneider here—sure—but that don't say—

DITRICH
(interrupting)
You're nuts. I never seen anybody here. How could I? I never been here before this.

COBBY

That being the case—what's to connect me with the Belletier job?

DITRICH

Somebody saw him—I don't know who—maybe you got a fink around. The little doctor's mug is all over the newspapers. Someone saw him here and went to the commissioner.

COBBY
(reaches for the bottle)
Sure you won't have one, Lieutenant?

DITRICH
(shakes his head)
Never drink when I'm on duty. It's against regulations.

COBBY

Look, Lieutenant. I got nothing to hide. Riedenschneider holed up there. He was broke. I let him use one of the upstairs rooms, for a couple of days. Then I got sick of having him around. I gave him a few bucks to get rid of him.

DITRICH

Where did he go?

COBBY

I don't know. I don't know.

DITRICH

Do you figure me for a pal, Cobby—or don't you?

COBBY

I sure do, Lieutenant.

DITRICH

Then take my advice and turn state's! We'll make ourselves a little deal with the commissioner. You won't get more than a year or two.

COBBY

Look, Lieutenant. I'm clean. I don't know where the Doc went. That's the truth.

DITRICH

They won't believe you at Headquarters, Cobby. Every time you'd tell 'em that—they'd work you over. And you ain't the type that can take it. Believe me, you'd spill your guts in half an hour.

Every nerve in Cobby's body begins to jump.

COBBY
(begging)

Give me a break. You came to make a pinch—fine—but I'm not here. I had to go to Chi on business.

DITRICH

No, Cobby. You're right here.

COBBY

I've always treated you right, Lieutenant. Let me duck out. You can get away with that.

DITRICH

No. I couldn't. The commissioner's mad—he's out for blood. It's not going to be mine.

COBBY
(hysterically)

You're not gonna stop me! You're gonna let me go! You're gonna do that—if you don't—

DITRICH

Yeah. I know. You'll give me the finger.

COBBY

That's right. I'll tell them you saw Riedenschneider here and didn't roust him—why?—Because you'd've had to explain what you were doing here. I'll tell 'em about all the juice you been getting out of me.

DITRICH

Cobby, the only thing you're doing is making me sore.

COBBY
(shrilly)
Once I start singing I won't stop. They'll jug you right along side of me.

DITRICH

That's where you're wrong, Cobby. Even if they believe you it won't go too hard with me. Because I'll be the guy that cracked the biggest job ever pulled in the city.

Ditrich starts toward Cobby who retreats around the room until his back is to the door. Turning quickly, Cobby flings the door open. Ditrich backhands him a stunning, accurate blow. Cobby falls, still clinging to the door knob. Ditrich kicks the door shut. Cobby on all fours, tries to crawl away from Ditrich.

DITRICH

Look out, Cobby! Your're going to get hurt!

He yanks him to his feet, slaps him again.

COBBY

Ditrich, have you gone crazy? Look—it's Cobby! Your pal—Cobby!

DITRICH

Stand up!

Suddenly Cobby breaks down and begins to cry like a six-year-old.

DITRICH
(grinning)
I told you—you couldn't take it, Cobby.
(he pours whiskey into a glass)
—Here.

COBBY
(sobbing)
They'll call me a fink.

DITRICH
(puts a heavy arm around Cobby's shoulder)
That's my boy—
Cobby drinks.

DISSOLVE TO:

INT   MEDIUM SHOT   LIVING ROOM   EMMERICH'S COTTAGE
NIGHT
Emmerich is sitting on a chair, smoking a cigar, and talking. Angela
is sitting on the floor, clasping her knees, listening to him with
wide-eyed attention.

EMMERICH
—and as I'm pretty busy right now with lots of cases
coming up, I thought you might like to take a trip.

ANGELA
Where to?

EMMERICH
Oh—out to the coast—Florida—Anywhere you like.

ANGELA
Could I, Uncle Lon—anywhere—no fooling?

EMMERICH
I think a change of scene would do you good.

ANGELA
Wait—you wait right here. I've got the most terrific idea.
She runs out of the room, comes back with a travel magazine, opens
it to an illustrated page.

EMMERICH
Cuba—not a bad idea.

ANGELA
Imagine me on this beach—here. In my green bathing
suit—Yipe! I almost bought a white one the other day, but
it wasn't quite extreme enough—I mean—don't get me
wrong. If I really went in for the *extreme* extreme, I'd have
got a French suit. But run for your lives, girls—the fleet's
in! Oh, Uncle Lon, am I excited! Yipe!
O.S. the SOUND of the front door bell.

ANGELA
Oh heck! Look, Uncle Lon. Here's a French bathing suit.
You see? Doesn't she look indecent?

EMMERICH
Well, in an attractive sort of way.

ANGELA
Uncle Lon really! I'm surprised at you. No, I mean it. A
man of your education—and taste—and all. Nevertheless,
if you want me to—
O.S. the SOUND of loud knocking.

ANGELA
Who can that be? It's awfully late, isn't it?
(the knocking gets louder)
See who it is, Uncle Lon!
(he merely puffs at his cigar)
Why are they pounding so? I'm scared, Uncle Lon!
Emmerich gets up, walks out of the room.

CUT TO:

INT MEDIUM SHOT HALLWAY
Emmerich opens the door abruptly, and catches Andrews, the
homicide detective, with hand raised. Commissioner Hardy is
standing just beyond him—his overcoat collar turned up, and his
hat down almost over his eyes. Some distance behind Hardy are
two hulking harness-bulls.

EMMERICH
(to Andrews)
You must be a very hard-fisted young man . . . . Hello,
Hardy. Come on in. I've got a fire. You look cold.
Hardy and Andrews enter. Emmerich shuts the door in the faces of
the two policemen. CAMERA DOLLIES AHEAD OF THEM as he
leads the way into the living room. We get a fleeting glimpse of
Angela retreating down the hall toward her bedroom. Hardy goes to
the fireplace, and holds his hands out to the blaze.

HARDY
I'm here to arrest you, Emmerich.

EMMERICH
Mind telling me what for?

HARDY
Complicity.—In robbery and in murder.

EMMERICH
If I were you, Hardy, I'd dig up a few more charges
because that way you might be able to make one of them
stand up—providing you had an imbecile jury and the
right judge.

HARDY
(turns to Andrews)
Get the young lady.

ANDREWS
Yes, sir.
He moves quickly in the direction taken by Angela. Hardy takes a
document out of his pocket.

HARDY
It may interest you to know that your friend Cobby has
signed a confession. Want to take a look at it? Here . . .
He gives it to Emmerich who, after a long searching look into
Hardy's face, sits down in a chair, puts glasses on, and begins to
read.
CUT TO:

INT   HALLWAY
Andrews is knocking at Angela's locked door.

ANDREWS
(harshly)
Okay, miss. It's a shame to bust this door in—but here
goes—
It's unclocked, and opened at once. Andrews finds himself looking
into blazing yellow eyes as beautiful and as merciless as a wildcat's.
He recoils, snatching off his hat.

ANGELA
Haven't you bothered me enough you big . . . banana
head? Just try breaking my door in! Mr. Emmerich will
throw you out of the house.

ANDREWS
Afraid, not, miss. He's got troubles enough. In fact, he's a
dead duck.
O.S. the SOUND of Hardy's voice.

HARDY
(O.S.)

Hey, Andrews—hurry up. Bring the young woman in here!

ANGELA

Do I have to talk to him?
(changing her tune)
Why can't I just talk to you?

ANDREWS

Come on, baby, get it over with.—And be smart—tell the commissioner the truth. That's the only thing to do.

He takes her by the hand and leads her toward the living room.

CUT TO:

INT MEDIUM SHOT LIVING ROOM

Hardy is standing with his back to the fireplace, watching Emmerich reading Cobby's confession. The latter appears completely at ease. His feet are up on an ottoman. Andrews enters with Angela.

HARDY

Sit down!
(she obeys)
Andrews, repeat the statement Miss Finlay made before you and Officer Hannigan yesterday afternoon.

ANDREWS

She said: Mr. Emmerich was here—in this house with her from eleven-twenty p.m. to three a.m. last Friday night.

HARDY

(to Angela)
Is that the statement you made?

ANGELA

(in a small voice)
Yes, sir.

HARDY

(shouts angrily)
Is it true?

Angela stammers unintelligibly for a moment, then she looks at Emmerich for guidance. He rises and tosses his cigar into the fireplace, then he finishes his high-ball. For a moment, there is dead silence in the room except for the loud TICKING of a clock.

HARDY

You'd better think before you answer, young lady—unless you want to go to jail!

ANGELA

(gasps)

Jail!

HARDY

That's what happens to one who sets up a false alibi to keep another from being punished for a crime.

ANGELA

(weakly)

Mr. Emmerich wouldn't commit a crime.

HARDY

He would—and did.

Again the clock can he heard ticking.

EMMERICH

(lays Cobby's confession aside)

Tell them the truth.

ANGELA

(stammering)

Uncle Lon!

HARDY

There's nothing else to do unless you want to be indicted for obstructing justice.

ANGELA

What I said yesterday was—well—it was not exactly—I mean it wasn't really—

HARDY

(shouting)

Was it the truth?

ANGELA

(stammering)

No, sir.

HARDY

You weren't here with Emmerich were you?

ANGELA

No sir.

HARDY

You were someplace else and you were not with him!

ANGELA

Yes, sir.

HARDY

He told you exactly what to say—made you learn it by heart.

Angela suddenly doubles over, puts her head on her knees, and begins to cry bitterly.

HARDY

Answer me!

ANGELA

(sobbing)

I mean yes, sir—I mean I learned it by heart.

Hardy sighs and looks at Emmerich thoughtfully for a moment, then he turns to Andrews.

HARDY

Get a new statement from her. Have her sign it.

(to Angela)

—And this time, young lady, I want the whole truth.

ANDREWS

Yes, sir. Over here, Miss.

He indicates a desk in the far corner of the room. Passing Emmerich, Angela looks up at him with anguished eyes.

ANGELA

I . . . I tried . . . I'm sorry, Uncle Lon.

Emmerich smiles and nods.

EMMERICH

You did pretty well—considering.

Angela hesitates, then speaks in a low voice.

ANGELA

My trip, Uncle Lon—what about my trip?

EMMERICH
(shaking his head)
Some sweet kid.

Angela lowers her eyes and silently goes to the desk where she proceeds to dictate her statement.

HARDY
Seems to be all wrapped up, Emmerich.

Emmerich offers Hardy one of his Cuban cigars, but the commissioner refuses it.

HARDY
A little rich for my blood, thanks—like the rest of this place—and the blonde. I'm a hick at heart, Emmerich.

EMMERICH
(taking a cigar for himself)
Stop bragging, Hardy.
(he bites off the end)
By the way—You mind if I call my wife? She might be worrying about me. It's getting late.

HARDY
No. Help yourself.

EMMERICH
I prefer to call her in the card room—it's more private. Come along—if you like.

HARDY
No need for that. But don't try to run. You won't get very far.

INT   CARD ROOM
as Emmerich enters, sits down at the desk. Beyond him, in the light from the windows of the house, several policeman can be seen standing on the lawn outside, stamping to keep their feet warm. He picks up the phone, starts to dial, then changes his mind and hangs up. He sits staring at the floor for a moment. Remorse and defeat are written on his face. Then, tears springing to his eyes, he picks up a pen and writes swiftly on a memo pad.

INSERT: MEMO PAD

> Hardy:
>
> Don't disturb my wife till noon tomorrow.
> She is not well and needs her sleep.
>
> A.E.

CLOSE SHOT   EMMERICH
He reads the note over then, back to CAMERA, he leans down and
takes something from the bottom desk drawer. There is a sharp
report. He falls forward across the desk.

DISSOLVE

INT   FULL SHOT   STAIRWAY   CIAVELLI FLAT   SHOOTING
DOWN   MORNING
The lights are already out. A plainclothesman and a uniformed
officer come up the stairs toward CAMERA, which PANS WITH
THEM to the door. They take their guns out before knocking. The
door is immediately opened by a young priest.

DETECTIVE
We're looking for Louis Ciavelli.

FATHER SORTINO
Why, may I ask?

POLICEMAN
He's wanted for robbery, Father.

FATHER SORTINO
(recoiling slightly)
There must be some mistake.

DETECTIVE
Could be. But we've got our orders.

FATHER SORTINO
Louis Ciavelli is dead.
He opens the door wide enough for them to see the casket banked
with flowers against the parlor wall. The CAMERA ENTERS THE
ROOM, MOVES UP TO A CLOSE SHOT of Maria, who sits in a
rocking chair, dumb with grief. O.S. we hear the voices of the men
in the hall.

DETECTIVE
What did he die of?

FATHER SORTINO
A bullet wound—

DETECTIVE
Yeah?

FATHER SORTINO
—received in a street fight.

DETECTIVE
Street fight, eh?

FATHER SORTINO
I'd consider it a great favor if you didn't insist on going in.
Maria continues to rock in numb despair.

DISSOLVE TO:

MEDIUM LONG SHOT   CELL CORRIDOR AT HEADQUARTERS
TOWARD A SHORT, GROTESQUE MAN
being led forward between two heavy policemen: it's Gus Minissi.
Suddenly, Gus jerks back, hauling one of the policemen to his
knees, and without a word, turns back half a step to grab through
the bars of one of the cells, grappling fiercely and effectively with its
inmate—Cobby. It takes both officers to pull Gus off Cobby, but it
takes time and effort. Gus is almost carried in the grip of the two
policemen. When they are nearly the full length of the corridor, Gus
turns again to scream his curses back at Cobby.

GUS
You wait! You dirty fink! You ain't gonna live! You're
going the same place as your pal Emmerich! You wait! I'll
see you in the morgue!
The cops jerk him around the corner and out of sight, still scream-
ing.

DISSOLVE TO:

INT   FULL SHOT   DOLL'S APARTMENT   EVENING
Doc is cramming the lower lining of his overcoat with gems out of
the leather bag. Doll watches with amazement, turning occasionally
to look at Dix, who is standing up, reading the front page of a
newspaper.

DIX
(with contempt)
"Don't disturb my wife till noon tomorrow.
She's not well and needs her sleep.
A. E."
He throws the paper away.

DOC
(sweating as he works)
What foolishness!—Unbelievable! He wouldn't have got
more than two years.

DIX
Let's worry about us—not him.—How's your head, Doc?

DOC
Good as it ever was. Which isn't saying much.
Dix goes to the window and pulls the shade aside to look down into
the street.

DIX
Getting out of town is not going to be a cinch for you, Doc.
With your picture spread around.

DOC
Oh, I'll get out all right. I'll take a taxi to the edge of town,
and then have him drive me as far as Cleveland. Sure you
won't come along with me, Dix?

DIX
No, Doc.

DOC
If you won't come with me—will you finance me? I
haven't got but four or five dollars.

DIX
(readily)
Sure, I'll finance you.

DOC
I can get along on a thousand dollars, thanks very much,
and you can take your pick of the best stones—say maybe
fifty thousand dollars' worth.

DIX

What would I do with them? Can you see me walking into
a hock shop with stuff like that? First, they'd think I was a
phony, then they'd yell for the riot squad. No, Doc, you
can have the grand—but no rocks for me.
Dix takes his roll out and gives Doc the money.

DOC

Thank you, Dix. Tell me where to write you—at least I can
send you the five grand you got coming. What will your
address be in Kentucky?

DIX

Naw, Doc—forget it. Maybe I'll see you around.

DOC
(smiles sadly)
Well, goodbye then.

DIX

Goodbye, Doc—Hey, wait a minute—you haven't got a
heater. I'd let you have mine, but—
(he turns to Doll)
Got a gun, Doll?

DOLL

No, Dix. I used to have one around, but somebody stole it.

DOC

I don't want a gun—thank you. I haven't carried a gun
since my twenties. You carry a gun—you shoot a
policeman—a bad rap—hard to beat. You don't carry a
gun—you give up when they hold one on you.

DIX

All right, Doc, you know best.
Without another word, the little doctor goes softly out, closing the
door behind him. They listen to the squeak of his footsteps.

DOLL

How about some coffee, honey?

                         DIX
                    (ignoring her)
          That squarehead, he's a funny little guy. I don't get him at
          all.

                    `   DOLL
          Maybe because he's a foreigner. They don't think like us.
Dix goes to the window again, pulling aside the shade to watch Doc
cross the street and enter the darkness of a long alley.

                         DIX
          Anyway, he's got plenty guts.
Dix sits down again, the pain showing in his face.

                         DOLL
                    (again)
          How about some coffee, honey?

                         DIX
          Make it or shut up about it!
He gets up, walks several steps, puts out his hand to lean against a
wall, groaning involuntarily.

                         DOLL
                    (coming up beside him)
          It's that wound!

                         DIX
                    (gasping)
          Bright girl!

                         DOLL
          I know! Aspirin—
She rushes off to get the water and aspirin. Dix straightens himself
out on the floor, then turns over and gets to his feet. Doll comes back
with the glass of water and the little green bottle.

                         DOLL
          Here, honey. Take three—take four.
Dix swallows the aspirin, walks to the window once more, pulling
up the shade. The lights of the city lie beyond, joined by the arcs of
the bright lights over the river.

                         DOLL
          Lie down, Dix. Please lie down.

DIX

I got to get out of town too, Doll, and before morning.
He allows her to lead him over to the bed where he lies down.

DIX
(as though he were alone)
Yeah—the little Doc—is all right.

DISSOLVE TO:

EXT MEDIUM LONG SHOT A DESERTED SQUARE IN THE POORER SECTION OF TOWN NIGHT as seen past the exit from a narrow alley. Into the F.G., Doc Riedenschneider, his overcoat buttoned up over his neck, stops short as he emerges from the alley. Off to the right, two motorcycle cops are parked behind a hack stand, watching traffic. After a moment, Doc steps boldly forward and goes directly past the backs of the officers and into a cab.

INT MEDIUM SHOT CAB PROCESS Doc settles back with a cigar as the driver, a middle-aged man in a woolen cap, turns into the stream of traffic.

DOC
Pickering Avenue and Center Street. You know where that is?

DRIVER
Other side of town . . . .

DOC
How far is that?

DRIVER
I can make it in an hour.
The driver has a German accent, much more marked than Riedenschneider's.

DOC
(he sighs)
Okay. I got relatives living there. I'm between trains and I got nothing else to do.

DRIVER
I know how it is. I've got plenty of them. On both sides. Always writing me letters for money.
Doc looks at the photo of the driver opposite him. The name is Frank Schurz.

DOC

Haben sie Bekannten in Deutschland?
(Have you friends in Germany?)

DRIVER

Ach, ja! Sie sprechen gut Deutsch!
(Oh yes! You speak German well!)
They pass a police squad car. But it is nosing in toward a minor
accident and the taxi circles around it.

DOC

I haven't spoken German for a long, long time.

DRIVER

You have a München accent.

DOC

Yes, I was born there, but you know what they say. Home
is where the money is.
There's a pause; the traffic is thinning out.

DOC

Franz—how would you like to drive me to Cleveland?

DRIVER

That's a long way from here, my friend.

DOC

But it would still be quicker than to take the train tomorrow morning.

DRIVER

How about your relatives?

DOC

Forget 'em.

DRIVER

I don't know. Cleveland—that's a long way. Costs a lot of
money.

DOC

There's a fifty-dollar tip for you. What do you say?

DRIVER

For fifty dollars, I'd take you to the North Pole.
The taxi slows down, turning into a gas station. Through the glass
office, a motorcycle cop can be seen making a call by pay telephone.

                    DOC
What's the trouble, Franz?

                   DRIVER
If we're going to Cleveland, I better get gas.

                    DOC
Well, let's not stop here. Wait till we get out of town. Then
we can do everything at once: have a little meal—beer—a
cigar—and go in comfort.

                   DRIVER
I can see you're a man who likes his pleasures.
The driver drives his cab back into traffic again.

                    DOC
Well, Franz, what else is there in life, I ask you?
                                        DISSOLVE TO:

INT   DOLL'S APARTMENT   NIGHT
The lights are out.

MEDIUM CLOSE SHOT   DIX
leaning against the edge of the window, looking into the street
which is visible two stories down. Doll comes into view, crossing
the street in a hurry. Dix pulls down the shade, crosses the room
slowly, and turns on one of the lamps. There are rapid footsteps on
the stairs, the door is unlocked, and Doll enters, out of breath.

                    DIX
            (impatiently)
You've been gone nearly two hours. What happened?

                   DOLL
It took time. I was stopped twice—prowl cars. The neighborhood's just crawling with coppers. Dix, you can't
imagine—

                    DIX
All right! Did you get the car?

                   DOLL
Yes. Here's the change.
            (giving it to him)
It only came to four hundred dollars. I bought it from Big
Vivian. It's in pretty good shape, except the brakes need—

                    DIX
              (interrupting)
         Did you put gas in it?

                    DOLL
         Yes.

                    DIX
         Where did you park it?

                    DOLL
         Three blocks away.

                    DIX
         Good girl.
He's hidden the gun in a chair and now he picks it up, puts it in his
waistband. Then he grabs his coat, begins to put it on awkwardly,
painfully. Doll comes and helps him.

                    DOLL
         Dix—

                    DIX
         Yeah?

                    DOLL
         I'm scared. All those cops out there—

                    DIX
         They don't worry me one little bit. I'll drive slow. Head
         right down the main boulevard. In ten hours, I'm home,
         back home.
Having got on his coat, he goes heavily toward the door and unlocks
it and pulls it open. He looks back, not knowing how to say goodbye. Doll remains in the center of the room.

                    DOLL
         Dix—honey—how're you going to drive all that way?

                    DIX
         I'll make it.

                    DOLL
         No. Not in the shape you're in. Not in a million years.

DIX
(shouting)
I'll make it!
There's a pause for a moment. Doll looks down at the floor.

DOLL
(softly)
Then let me go with you.
Dix frowns, puzzled and disturbed.

DOLL
Please, Dix, please.

DIX
Are you crazy? I'm on the lam. Wanted bad. I'm packing heat—
(touching the gun in the waistband of his trousers, under the coat)

DIX
—and if there's any trouble, what good are you?

DOLL
I could drive.
Dix considers the idea for a moment.

DIX
(more quietly)
Doll, no. It don't make sense. They want me on a killing rap. You know what that means?

DOLL
I don't care. I want to be with you.

DIX
Well, I'll be a—

DOLL
You can't go without me. I won't let you.
She turns away from him, sitting down defiantly in a chair.

DOLL
(desperately)
I won't tell you where the car is.
Dix crosses the room and grabs her out of the chair. But the violence slowly goes out of him and he stands that way, with his fingers gripping her shoulders, looking at her.

                         DIX
                      (gently)
       I don't get it. I just don't get it.
Doll manages a small, triumphant smile.

                         DIX
         All right, kid. Get your things packed.

                                          DISSOLVE TO:

INT   FULL SHOT   A DINER ALONG THE ROAD TO
CLEVELAND   NIGHT   THROUGH THE WINDOWS A PORTION OF
THE HIGHWAY ILLUMINATED BY THE FLOODLIGHTS OF A FILLING
STATION ACROSS THE WAY
In the F.G., a girl of about sixteen, with a plump, pretty face, is
dancing with a tall boy in a checkered shirt and jeans. Another boy,
much shorter, is watching them, leaning on the table of their booth.
At the counter, Riedenschneider and the cab driver. Schurz, are
finishing their hamburgers and beer. The music ends; the girl
dances a couple of beats more, and then stops. Doc still watches.

                         GIRL
       More, more!

                      TALL BOY
       I'm fresh out of nickels, Jeannie. How about you, Red?

                         Red
                   (the shorter boy)
       I'm always fresh out.

                         GIRL
       Well, get some!

                      TALL BOY
       Say, you know you cost a guy a lot of money!

                         GIRL
       Nickels he's complaining about! What a spender!
Doc glances behind him to look at the girl again.

The girl still complains to the two boys, who look away from her,
sulking, drinking the ice-water left in their exhausted Cokes.

                         GIRL
       Sure, he wants a date. He always wants a date. But has he
       got a car? No. He's got to bring his chum, Red, along

because chum Red's got a car if you can call it a car! Where
do we go? To a third-run movie. Then we take a ride and
blow two tires. Not one—two. Then we come in here and
he treats me to what? Cokes! And I can't even listen to
records in spite of the fact that my old man is going to
whale me when I come in this time of night—but good!

DOC
(turning to the counterman)
Would you have change for a dollar—in nickels, please?
The counterman nods, opens the cash register, takes out a bank
package of nickels.

GIRL
At least you could dig down for enough to play me some
music!

RED
Aw, Jeannie! Cut it out!
Doc has torn open the roll of nickels, and now he turns on the stool
and crosses the booth where the two boys and the girl are arguing.

DOC
Excuse me, boys and girls. But I like music, too. Miss—
(turning to the girl)
—will you play a tune for me?

GIRL
I sure will. What do you like?

DOC
You pick them.
(he pours out the nickels on the table)

GIRL
But gee—gosh! How many nickels you got there?

DOC
Not very many. Play what you like.

GIRL
Gee—okay!
The girl picks up five nickels and puts them into the jukebox. It
lights up, bubbling in its colored tubes. The girl begins to dance, all
by herself, even before the music begins. Riedenschneider watches
her.

SEVERAL CLOSE SHOTS   RIEDENSCHNEIDER   INTERCUT WITH

SEVERAL CLOSE SHOTS   THE GIRL DANCING
sometimes with the tall boy, sometimes swinging off alone, brush-
ing past Doc's knees as he watches.

INT   FULL SHOT   THE DINER   NIGHT
The driver has swallowed the last of his beer. He looks at
Riedenschneider, a little puzzled and upset by what's happening.

DRIVER
It's getting late. Maybe we better be moving along.

DOC
(not taking his eyes off the girl)
Plenty of time, my friend, plenty of time.

MEDIUM CLOSE SHOT   THE GIRL DANCING
intensely conscious of Doc in the F.G., CAMERA PANS with her as
she moves.

DRIVER
(O.S.)
Look, Mister—it's a long way to Cleveland.
The girl begins to dance back in the direction of Doc, but the CAMERA CONTINUES TO PAN for a second, STOPPING with the broad back of a man at the cigarette counter, paying for a couple of packs. From the Sam Browne belt, the uniform, and the gun in its holster, he is recognizable as a state policeman. Receiving his change, he turns to go, glances briefly at the girl, then at Doc, who raises his napkin and turns his face away.

INT   MEDIUM SHOT   DINER
The state policeman goes on out of the diner. The record runs out, and the girl finishes her dance with a pose, glancing over her shoulder at Doc.

MEDIUM CLOSE SHOT   DOC AND THE GIRL

DOC
(regretfully)
Well, I suppose we better go.

GIRL
Don't go. We haven't used the nickels.
She smiles toward him, showing as many pretty teeth as possible.

DOC
(buttoning his overcoat)
You use them.

GIRL
Gee, thanks. It's sure nice of you.

DOC
Don't mention it.
The girl escorts him to the door of the diner. The state policeman has mounted his motorcycle, and, joined by a fellow officer, is leaving the diner for the dark highway beyond. Doc notes this fact out of the corner of his eye.

GIRL
(softly, as she shakes hands with him)
Goodbye. And thanks. Thanks ever so much.

DOC

The pleasure was all mine.

Schurz opens the door, and they go out.

EXT   MEDIUM SHOT   THE HALF-LIGHTED AREA IN FRONT OF THE
DINER   NIGHT

Riedenschneider and Schurz get into the cab, the Doc looking back
through the rear window to smile once more at the girl smiling
through the window of the diner. The cab pulls away toward the
highway.

INT   MEDIUM SHOT   CAB (PROCESS)

PAST Doc in the F.G. and PAST the driver and THROUGH the
windshield as they swing out onto the road. Clearly visible in front
of them are the two state policemen on their motorcycles, one
consulting with the other. Then suddenly, they swing around and
move in the opposite direction and toward the cab. As they come
forward, they motion to the cab driver to stop. He obeys.

EXT   MEDIUM SHOT   A SECTION OF STATE HIGHWAY   NIGHT

The first cop, the one who had glanced at Doc in the diner, comes
forward with drawn automatic and pulls open the door of the cab.
The scene is illuminated in the two brilliant headlights of the
parked motorcycles.

DOC

You men want something?

FIRST COP

What do you think, Ed?

SECOND COP

Might be the number one boy. Just might be.

SCHURZ

Say, what is this?

SECOND COP

Better frisk him.

Doc hands his overcoat to Schurz.

DOC

Go right ahead—
            (as the cop frisks him)
You must have me mixed up with somebody else. I'm

from Cleveland—the importing business. My name's
Klemper.

The first cop has gone over him, found nothing but a roll of bills,
which he fingers and then puts back in Doc's pocket.

FIRST COP
Nothing here. Let's see that coat, hackie.

He takes the overcoat from Schurz's arm, goes through the pockets
with minute care. They're all empty. He throws the coat back to
Schurz.

SCHURZ
Hey, you're making a big mistake. This guy's—

FIRST COP
(interrupting)
Keep out of this, hackie.

SECOND COP
Tell you what. Let's phone the city and check on the
description.

The first cop nods, waits till the second cop has drawn his automatic, then walks heavily toward the diner. Doc looks after him.

SECOND COP
Don't move, feller. Just stay where you are with your back
to me.

DOC
Of course.

As, somewhere in the pool of light in the B.G., the door of the diner
is opened when the policeman enters once more, there's the
SOUND of music from the jukebox, and over it, the girl's high-
pitched laughter. Doc remains, however, with his back to this
scene.

DOC
Excuse me, officer. But will you tell me something?

SECOND COP
Maybe. But just keep the eyes front.

DOC
How long have you been out here?

                    SECOND COP
That's a darn funny question.

                        DOC
        (he shrugs)
It's not important.

                    SECOND COP
We've been watching you through that window for two,
three minutes.

                        DOC
Ah—yes. Say about as long as it takes to play a phono-
graph record . . . .

                    SECOND COP
How's that again? What are you talking about?

                        DOC
It doesn't matter.

                    SECOND COP
Keep your face front.

                        DOC
        (obeying)
Do you mind if I smoke a cigar?

                    SECOND COP
Just stand still mister—we'll talk about smoking a cigar
later.

                        DOC
Certainly, officer, certainly.

                                    DISSOLVE TO:

EXT   MEDIUM TWO-SHOT   PROCESS   DOLL'S CAR   NIGHT
SHOOTING THROUGH THE WINDSHIELD TOWARD DOLL AND DIX.
Dix is behind the wheel, Doll seated beside him. The car is not
moving: they're at a grade crossing, waiting for a long, slow freight
to pass. They watch in silence.

INT   MEDIUM CLOSE TWO-SHOT   DOLL'S CAR
behind Doll and Dix and toward the dark masses of freight cars as
they move slowly by.

DOLL
How are you feeling now, Dix?

DIX
All right. Cold. It didn't use to get cold, this time of the year.

DOLL
Dix, why don't you let me drive for a while?
There's a pause before Dix answers.

DIX
You don't know the way. I'd just have to keep telling you.

DOLL
Is it much longer, Dix?
He doesn't answer. Beyond them, the black freight cars roll ominously forward and past. Slowly, Dix leans forward, his head slumping on the wheel and pressing on the horn. Doll is terrified. She tries to rouse him, but fails. His face is dead white, his eyes open. She gets out, runs in front of the car, cries out for help to the slowly moving, inexorable train, a cry rather than any specific word. The tail end of the train rolls by. She goes back into the car, moving Dix to one side so she can drive. He falls over, partly on the floor, partly on the seat. She starts the car, drives across the tracks, enters the outskirts of a small town, closed, dark, with empty streets. Driving frantically, almost haphazardly, she sees a man walking along the sidewalk, and slows down the car beside him. He's a man of about forty, a railroad switchman in overalls and railroad cap.

DOLL
Mister—can you help me? We need a doctor, bad. My husband's sick.
The switchman comes up to the car, lifts up Dix, who moans faintly.

SWITCHMAN
(getting in the car)
Come on. I'll show you.—go straight on, ma'am—to the end of the block.
Doll obeys.

SWITCHMAN

We'll get Doc Swanson. Lives right near—on Elm Street.—There—that's Elm, turn right, ma'am.— Recognize it by that big tree.—Now—it's the second house—that one coming up.

She stops with a lurch before a huge, dark house with the gold sign: Doctor A. A. Swanson, M.D.

EXT   MEDIUM LONG SHOT   A RESIDENTIAL STREET IN A SMALL TOWN   NIGHT

as Doll gets out of the car, runs up the walk, up the porch steps, and knocks at the door of the dark house. There's no response, and she goes to a window and raps on the glass. A light goes on, far inside the house, and then the hall light, and finally there are footsteps, and the door opens. The doctor is still in pajamas, with thin, tousled grey hair.

DOCTOR SWANSON

Well, now! What's the trouble?

DOLL

He's sick. Fainted.

DOCTOR

Who?

DOLL

My husband—while we were driving. He's in the car.

DOCTOR

Well, let's get him up here. Where I can look at him.

He starts to go down the steps, retreats, pulls on a pair of shoes, crosses the porch and down the short path. The switchman and Doll have managed to lift Dix out of the car, and now all three of them bring him, still unconscious, through the open door of the house and into the examination room.

INT   FULL SHOT   DR. SWANSON'S EXAMINATION ROOM   NIGHT

as Dix is lifted onto the examining table. The Doc listens to his heart, his pulse. Then he goes and washes his hands at the sink.

DOCTOR

Get his coat and shirt off.

Doll obeys, helped by the switchman. The doctor goes to a table, to

A Screenplay 137

prepare a bottle of plasma for transfusion. Doll in the F.G., strokes Dix's face and hair. He is still unconscious, though sometimes his lips move without a sound.

> DOCTOR
> Man's been hemorrhaging. Lost a lot of blood. What happened?

> DOLL
> He was hurt—in the right side. He was in an auto accident.

> DOCTOR
> Um. Yes. How long's that wound been let go?

> DOLL
> Couple of days.—Is it bad, Doctor? I mean, real bad?

> DOCTOR
> It isn't good, ma'am.
> (coming up with the plasma)
> Got a good strong arm, Mr. Atkinson?

> SWITCHMAN
> Good as any, Doc. I guess.

> DOCTOR
> Hold this for me.

He gives him the plasma bottle to hold in the air, while he inserts the needle in Dix's arm. Doll inhales sharply, then bites her lip. The doctor leaves, going into an adjacent room and shutting the door. But he can be heard clearly, picking up the phone. Doll turns her head, listening.

> DOCTOR
> (O.S.)
> Hello—let me talk to Tom. This is Dr. Swanson. Well, wake him up.

In the F.G., Dix's head moves, he grunts, then pulls himself up on one elbow.

> DIX
> Gimme a drink—I'm thirsty.

                           DOLL
        Sure, Dix, sure. Lie down, sweetheart. Please lie down.
Dix turns on his elbow, looking toward the closed door of the
adjacent room.

                          DOCTOR
                          (O.S.)
        Hello, Sheriff? Listen, Tom, got a man here with a gunshot
        wound. Pretty bad.
Dix turns to look at the switchman, who says nothing, just holds the
plasma bottle, his railroad cap still on.

                           DIX
        Who's that?

                           DOLL
        Dix—I had to take you to the doctor! I couldn't help it!

                          DOCTOR
                          (O.S.)
        Hold him?—Don't have to. The man's unconscious. No,
        he's a stranger to me.—His wife's with him. Says it was an
        auto accident.
Dix sits up, pulls the needle out of his arm, drops from the table. His
knees bend, but he gets hold of himself and stumbles out, into the
hall, and across the porch. Doll runs after him, supporting him. The
switchman doesn't move, still holding the bottle in the air.

EXT   MEDIUM SHOT   FRONT SEAT OF DOLL'S CAR   NIGHT
as Dix comes toward it, pulls himself under the steering wheel, and
grimacing with pain starts the car. Doll, terrified, climbs in beside
him.

INT   FULL SHOT   THE EXAMINATION ROOM   NIGHT
as Doctor Swanson emerges, and seeing the patient gone, runs to
the window.
                                                    CUT TO:

EXT   MEDIUM CLOSE SHOT   DOLL'S CAR   NIGHT
as Dix shifts directly into second, presses his foot down on the
accelerator. The car responds with a roar, and lurches forward,
away from camera.

A Screenplay

CUT TO:

INT   FULL SHOT   THE EXAMINATION ROOM   NIGHT
as Doctor turns toward the switchman, who has put down the
plasma bottle and is filling his pipe.

> DOCTOR
> (dumbfounded)
> Where they going?

> SWITCHMAN
> I don't know, Doc.

> DOC
> Why'd you let him?

> SWITCHMAN
> Wasn't any of my business.

> DOCTOR
> Well, he won't get very far. That's for sure. He hasn't got
> enough blood left in him to keep a chicken alive.

CUT TO:

EXT   MEDIUM LONG SHOT   SMALL TOWN STREET   NIGHT
seen past Dix's white face and through the dusty windshield of
Doll's car as it shoots forward. It wavers dangerously for a moment,
and as it gathers more and more speed, races down the street and
out of town along the main highway. At a fearful, rocking speed,
the wheels of the car straddle the white center line that comes
curving up out of the darkness.

DISSOLVE TO:

INT   HARDY'S OFFICE   JUST AT DAWN   MEDIUM CLOSE
SHOT   HARDY AT HIS DESK
He's been at work all night, and he looks it.

> HARDY
> Are there any more questions?

CAMERA MOVES BACK into a FULL SHOT OF THE ROOM. It's
crowded with fifteen or twenty police reporters, sitting on the few
chairs or leaning against the walls of the tiny office.

REPORTER
I don't like to harp on the same point, Commissioner, but what about Ditrich? If the past of this police department is any precedent—

HARDY
Lieutenant Ditrich is in jail, and he'll go to trial. He'll be tried by a jury of twelve citizens—the people for whom he was working. Let them show justice or compassion, as they see fit.

REPORTER
What would be your verdict, Commissioner?

HARDY
I'm not sure. I'm not sure at all.
(he walks around the desk and among the reporters, pausing occasionally as he talks, to look a man straight in the face)
Let me put it this way. It's nothing strange that there are corrupt officers in the police department. There would have to be. People are people, even in blue uniform. The dirt they are trying to clean up is bound to soil them a little. They can become brutal, grafting, weak, inefficient. But not all of them. Not one in ten, nor one in a hundred. The ordinary patrolman is an honest man doing an honest job. Look here—
Hardy goes to a battery of four small loudspeakers, switches on the first channel. A woman's voice is giving coded information.

HARDY
Listen.—I know you're police reporters, and you hear this all day long. But I want you to listen with your conscience—not just your ears.
He switches on a second channel, overlapping the first.

HARDY
We send police assistance to every one of these calls. Because they're not just code numbers on a radio beam. They're cries for help: people are being cheated—robbed, murdered, raped—
(switching on a third channel)

And it goes on twenty-four hours a day—
(switching on a fourth channel)
—Every day in the year. And that's not exceptional, that's usual. And it's the same in every city in the modern world. CAMERA MOVES ON PAST HARDY TOWARD the back of four small loudspeakers, each with its lights flashing underneath. The babble of voices, as the CAMERA COMES CLOSE, is sinister and frightening.

HARDY
(O.S.)
But suppose we had no police force—good or bad. Suppose we had—
(he switches off all four channels)
—just silence.
CAMERA MOVES BACK to include Hardy and the reporters.

HARDY
No one to listen.—No one to answer, the war is finished. The jungle wins. The criminals take over.—Think about it.
Hardy walks back behind his desk. Beyond him, the city glints and smokes in the first light of day.

HARDY
Well, gentlemen. Three men are in jail—three dead, one by his own hand, and one man is a fugitive, and we've reason to think, badly wounded. Six out of seven, that's not bad. But we'll get the last one too. In many ways he's the most dangerous of them all. A hardened killer, a hooligan, a man without human feeling or human mercy.
DISSOLVE TO:

EXT   LONG SHOT   THE BRIDGE OVER A WIDE, CLEAR RIVER
SUNRISE
CAMERA PANS WITH Doll's car as it crosses the bridge, emerges at eighty miles per hour, into rolling farm country.

INT   MEDIUM SHOT   THE FRONT SEAT OF DOLL'S CAR   DAY
PROCESS
Dix is still driving, his fists gripped to the wheel. The car has not slackened its terrible speed. Doll holds on to the dashboard, the

handle of the door, paralyzed with fear. Dix's face no longer looks
ill: it looks lively, keen, except that he breathes through his mouth
like a winded animal. His voice, when he speaks, has a curious,
clear, fresh quality.

                    DIX
I tell you, the black one's the best. The bay is all right, but
the black is a real good colt. Prettiest way of going of
anything Pa ever bred—easy as thank you, but he's always way out in front of the other yearlings. I sure hope Pa
don't sell him. He's a stake horse or I never saw one. That
black colt will win Pa out of debt if he only hangs on to
him.

                    DOLL
          (sobbing)
Dix, honey!—Oh, dear God—what am I going to do?

                    DIX
I said it, and I'll say it again. If Pa just hangs on to that
black colt everything's going to be all right.
He stops the car.

                    DIX
          Here we are!
She looks away from him, and off to the right, where a rich land-
scape of rolling farm country extends to the horizon, white houses
set in the valleys and connected by lines of fences or trees set in
order between fields. Then her eye falls on a name carved into the
gate: Hickorywood Farm.

EXT   MEDIUM SHOT   DOLL'S CAR ON THE COUNTRY ROAD
EARLY MORNING
Dix gets out of the car, and before Doll can look back, he's gone to a
gate in the fence and pulled it open. He goes through, closing it
behind him. Doll runs around the car to stay with him, but she has
trouble getting the gate open again, for it has to be lifted over the
stones heaped around the post. He strides directly through a field of
lush Kentucky grasses. He's ten paces ahead of her.

EXT   MEDIUM SHOT   THE FIELD   EARLY MORNING
There are ten or fifteen thoroughbreds off toward a distant fence.
Dix strides, almost at a running pace, leaving a path through the
grass. Doll, still wearing high-heeled shoes, stumbles as she tries to
catch up with him.

DOLL

Dix—wait!

Suddenly, as though someone has pulled a string inside of him, he falls down. Doll runs up to him.

DOLL

Dix!—

MEDIUM TWO-SHOT DOLL AND DIX
His face lies in the grass. He murmurs inaudibly. Doll puts her hands under him and turns him over. His life is ebbing.

DOLL

Dix!—Dix!—Dix!

Then she lets go of him, sobbing, and gets to her feet and runs, uphill, the CAMERA PANNING TO FOLLOW HER. Over the crest of the hill, very distant, a man is mowing hay with a team. She screams toward him.

DOLL

Mister!—Mister!—Mister!

MEDIUM CLOSE SHOT DIX, FACE UPWARD, EYES OPEN, DEAD ON THE GROUND

DOLL

(O.S. distant)

Mister!—Wait!

Then her voice is no longer audible. There's a second of perfect silence, then a peculiar shadow moves over the grass and over Dix's body and across his face. It's the shadow of a horse, and now a big bay gelding walks slowly toward him, lowering his head to look at Dix. Another horse, full of their peculiar slow curiosity, comes up too. And then, still other horses move toward the group, and they stand there, looking down at the dead human face, watching with infinite patience.

FADE OUT:

END

Afterword
By W. R. Burnett

The Asphalt Jungle appeared on American movie screens nearly thirty years ago, so it took me a while to gather my thoughts about it. Quite a few of my novels and stories have been turned into motion pictures, but not one of them pleased me as much as *The Asphalt Jungle*, neither *Little Caesar* nor *High Sierra*. Luckily *The Asphalt Jungle* fell into good hands. Dore Schary, then the head of production at Metro-Goldwyn-Mayer, decided to try a crime-action picture after several of his pictures of a different type did poorly for him. He bought *The Asphalt Jungle* from me in manuscript. It was later published by Alfred Knopf.

Strangely enough, Schary turned the property over to Arthur Hornblow to make; Hornblow was then a contract producer at MGM. It was hardly Hornblow's cup of tea—he had built his reputation with a far different type of picture. But Hornblow made the correct move and hired John Huston to write the screenplay (with Ben Maddow) and direct the picture; and apparently he gave Huston his head. Huston is an adept at putting a property he likes on the screen—how to dramatize its essence, what it is really saying. And this he did very successfully with *The Asphalt Jungle*. He stayed close to the characters, the action, and the atmosphere. Nothing was invented, nor was the story changed in any respect. Not that I agreed entirely with what was done. We met at my house several times for conferences, but it is hard to win an argument with Huston. In my opinion, Huston took off the frame. I wanted to start the picture just as it was started in the novel, with the horrific news of the nightly toll of crime coming in over the Commissioner's radio, the voice of the asphalt jungle, as the Commissioner delivers a needed lesson to the newsmen. Instead, the picture starts as any small-time crime story might start: night, slums, an individual pursuing his individual way. Nor was I happy with the end of Dix Handley, the Southern strong-arm heister—half dead, but chasing horses around in a field. This was overdramatization.

Aside from those two points, I was satisfied with everything else in the film; and I think it is without a doubt one of the best films of its genre. It was artistically successful, and imitated for years afterwards. Even the word "jungle"—used in the sense I used it—appeared in title after title. Our film had a strong impact on movie-making.

Sadly enough, MGM had no experience in marketing such a picture, and they bungled it, where Warner's would have succeeded heavily with it, as they did with *Little Caesar* and *High Sierra*. How to sell it as a major picture! To MGM a "crime" picture was not a major picture. A Garbo picture was a major picture to them. To complicate matters, exhibitors wrote claiming they didn't understand the title—what did it mean? This is hard to believe, but true. So for a while the title was changed to the "Pelletier Jewel Robbery"—I cringe when I think about it. But eventually things got straightened out, and I believe that the picture did well enough commercially. It should have been a blockbuster.

Artistically, it holds up very well and doesn't seem dated at all though it appeared first in 1950. The casting was excellent: Sam Jaffe, Sterling Hayden, Marc Lawrence, Tony Caruso, James Whitmore, and the others all seemed to me like the variegated characters I visualized originally. The direction, in general, couldn't have been improved. I've had uncomfortable experiences in thirty years in Hollywood, but this was certainly not one of them.

How MGM operates now, I don't know—but for many years, decades, its system and its outlook remained the same. It was the glamour studio, specializing in elaborate and expensive vehicles tailored for its stable of stars, and in large-scale musicals, which we all took in stride in those days, not overly impressed. But since their recent re-release we now realize they were cinematic masterpieces. I bring this up because in the early thirties I had an experience at MGM similar to my experience with *The Asphalt Jungle*.

Irving Thalberg wanted a large crime story—to compete with the success Warner Brothers was having with *Little Caesar, The Public Enemy,* and others. I wrote one for him, called *The Beast of the City*. It was made on a very large scale, with Walter Huston, Jean Hersholt, and Jean Harlow. But when it was finished, as with *The Asphalt Jungle*, they didn't know what to do with it, how to market it; and, unlike *The Asphalt Jungle*, it died. It is hardly known at all. But I saw it run off lately at the American Film Institute, and in my opinion it is one of the best, if not the best movie, of the whole crime cycle of the day. It was released in 1934, I believe, and has hardly been heard from since, and then only because a young movie critic and expert dug it out and ran it off for me. I thought this might be of some interest to movie buffs—and the country is full of them at present.

Textual Note

The screenplay published here is the mimeographed OK Script dated 10-12-49. Punctuation has been regularized; but no substantive emendations have been made in dialogue. The name of the jewelry store, given in the mimeographed screenplay as both *Belletier's* and *Pelletier's*, has been regularized to *Belletier's*.

3.24–25	block, enters	[	block and enters
27.11	whomever	[	whoever
60.7	gently	[	gentle

W. R. Burnett is a novelist and screenwriter. Among his awards is the Screen Writers' Award for best drama in 1963 for *The Great Escape*. His novels include *Little Caesar, High Sierra*, and *The Roar of the Crowd*.

John Huston received the Screen Director's Guild Award for his direction of *The Asphalt Jungle*. Writer, actor, director, his credits include such classics as *The Maltese Falcon* and *The Treasure of The Sierra Madre*.

Ben Maddow is a novelist, screenwriter, and biographer. His *Edward Weston: Fifty Years, an Illustrated Biography* was nominated for a National Book Award. Among his screenplays are *Intruder in the Dust, The Unforgiven*, and *The Secret of Santa Vittoria*.